# THE TRUEST FAN BLUEPRINT

# THE TRUEST FAN BLUEPRINT

FOCUS ON WHAT MATTERS TO
ACHIEVE YOUR MOST CHERISHED GOALS

ROB BROWN

MIRASEE PRESS
5750 Avenue Notre Dame de Grace
Montreal, Quebec
H4A 1M4, Canada
www.mirasee.com



Hardback ISBN: 978-1-7373742-7-5
Paperback ISBN: 978-1-7373742-6-8
E-Book ISBN: 978-1-7373742-8-2
LCCN: 2023912266

Printed in the United States of America
1 3 5 7 9 10 8 6 4 2

*Dedicated to Lori, my wife and my rock,*
*thank you for always being my Truest Fan.*
*I love you more than words can express.*

# CONTENTS

# INTRODUCTION

**WELCOME,** and thank you for picking up your copy of *The Truest Fan Blueprint*! I'm excited to share with you the blueprint that I use to coach financial and service professionals who are business owners, entrepreneurs, and industry leaders. I've helped all these people to live their best lives with intentionality and authenticity.

If you haven't had a chance to read my first book and aren't familiar with the term "Truest Fan," let me take a moment to explain. Our Truest Fans are those cheerleaders who want nothing but the best for us—and I believe that we are all called to be Truest Fans for ourselves and for others. Imagine a world where we all cheered each other on—we could solve a lot of problems, not just in business and family challenges, but in all aspects of life.

If you invest the time and energy to follow the blueprint outlined in this book, your life and the lives of those around you will be better, your businesses will grow, the causes you care about will flourish, your family will be happier, and you'll have a closer relationship with God. If we live to love and serve others, and to lead where we have opportunities, we will live with greater purpose and make a greater impact, both in making small differences and in moving mountains.

Let me introduce myself. First and foremost, I am a follower of Jesus, and I believe in the importance of loving God and loving others as ourselves. The Truest Fan mission is just another way of restating those great commandments and applying them in a practical way. I'm also a husband to Lori, a father of triplet daughters, and a grandfather. My family is incredibly important to me, and I hope that they see these lessons as a way that I try to live my life and instill values in them to be the best at whatever they do.

In addition, I am a coach, consultant, and speaker, and I co-host the *Truest Fan Blueprint* podcast with my business partner, Phil Calandra. I work with entrepreneurs and business owners, many of whom are in the financial services industry. I've spent almost my entire career working inside financial services companies or beside financial planners, advisors, and registered investment advisors. In my coaching work, I use the exact same strategies that I teach in this book. My greatest accomplishments in my work come from seeing my clients put their dreams into action and start to live with greater purpose and impact. When my clients start following Truest Fan principles, it improves their businesses, their families, and the causes they care about—whether we're trying to grow revenues or profits, build stronger teams, create succession plans, or develop marketing and sales strategies.

I work with a select group of clients on a one-to-one basis, as well as speak at and lead group or cohort programs that are modeled on the ideas of a Truest Fan Roundtable—which you'll learn more about in this book! I hope that as we journey together through the Truest Fan Blueprint, you'll join me in being a Truest Fan and living your life with greater purpose and impact.

Before we delve into the blueprint, I want to tell you about my previous book, *Truest Fan: Live, Love, and Lead with Purpose and Impact*. The book was a huge success, and I was thrilled to hear from readers who put the seven lessons I taught in that book to work in their lives. These lessons helped them become better parents, siblings, friends, volunteers, and businesspeople:

1. To be a Truest Fan, you must be your own Truest Fan.
2. To be a Truest Fan, you must learn to put your most important work first and avoid anything that may get in the way.
3. Love one another because, no matter whether you win or lose, life is about the way you play the game.
4. Smiles and kind words go a long way. When you're a Truest Fan, you're always on duty.
5. Your family deserves your very best.
6. You are never alone; God is your Truest Fan.
7. Intentionally live the life you were intended to live.

After publishing *Truest Fan*, I wanted to get a little deeper, with advice for how readers can *take action* on these principles. I also received many questions from readers about how to apply the seven principles of being a Truest Fan to a business setting. That was the impetus for writing this book. *The Truest Fan Blueprint* is a parable that introduces Tito, a wise diner owner and mentor figure, and the roundtable he helps establish consisting of Grant, Nuria, and Bo.

As you follow along on these four characters' journeys, you'll learn how to put the Truest Fan lessons into practice yourself in a business setting, whether you're an entrepreneur, business owner, industry leader, or just getting started on your journey. You'll discover how to prioritize your most important work, build strong relationships with your colleagues, and create a positive impact in your business and community.

You can read this book in two ways. You can read it the whole way through and then go back and begin implementing the ideas, or you can implement the ideas as you go. Each section has a stopping point with simple instructions on how to implement the strategy that's been discussed. You'll find pages in those spots where you can complete the exercises. This is a book that's meant to be highlighted, underlined, and written in. Don't be afraid to write in the margins.

I encourage you to approach this book with an open mind and a willingness to take action. As you read, think about how you can apply the lessons to your own life and business. Don't be afraid to experiment and try new things. I'm rooting for your success and doing everything I can to support you along the way—because I am your Truest Fan.

CHAPTER 1

# ALONE IN THE CROWD

## NURIA'S AWAKENING

**NURIA SAT** at her desk, staring at her computer screen in utter despair. For what must have been the hundredth time, she scanned the words of the email she'd just received from one of her most valued clients—now an ex-client.

"We expected more of you," it read. "You've really let us down."

Thinking back, Nuria could picture herself during the contract-signing meeting with this client, a tiny startup called Erickson Inc. At the time, it was her single largest account, and she'd been so proud and excited as she shook Mr. Erickson's hand. She could even recall saying, "I will never let you down."

But now, years later, she had let him down. True, she'd delivered her work on time, but there'd been no imagination, no creativity, and she knew he was right to fire her. As she scrolled through the email chain, Nuria noticed something that made her heart sink even lower—every message she had sent to Mr. Erickson lately had been a reply. Not once had she reached out with a new idea or proactive support.

She buried her face in her hands, feeling overwhelmed and exhausted.

"Is this really the way you want to live?" said a voice from deep inside her. "Always playing defense, not finding any joy in your work, wondering when the next client will abandon you? Life at home is strained, too. You can't even remember the last time you had a real vacation. Maybe you should quit and start something new."

Nuria's heart raced at the thought. Quit? Start something new? Though it sounded tempting, she hated the thought of throwing away what she had built. She looked around her office, at the pictures of her family and friends and clients, at the awards and accolades on the walls. Building the Custom Design Group, a highly respected website design company, had been her life's work. CDG had once been on the who's who lists of both the fastest-growing web design firms and the top places to work in the city. Was she really willing to give it up? Wouldn't she be admitting defeat?

Something had to change. Nuria knew she couldn't keep working this way, running herself ragged trying to keep up with the demands of her clients as well as battling to find new business opportunities. She needed to come up with a new strategy that would help her build a stronger, more sustainable, more enjoyable business.

Nuria took a deep breath and stood up from her desk. She walked over to the window that overlooked her team, nearly fifty of them now hard at work in different areas of the open-plan office. Their energy and the thought of the many incredible projects they had completed together started to wipe away her feelings of despair.

Nuria realized suddenly that when she had first founded CDG, she'd had big dreams about the future. She absolutely knew why she was passionate about web design, and who she would be doing it for. And she saw the impact she could make if she were successful. That sense of purpose had been her driving motivation. These days, though? There was so much to do that she barely thought about the bigger picture anymore. She wondered how she could recapture that sense of wonder and adventure.

"I'll make a plan," she said aloud to the empty office. "I'll figure out exactly what my next steps should be, and soon I'll start feeling motivated again."

But just as Nuria returned to her desk, her inner voice spoke up again.

"You cannot do this alone," it screamed. "That's how you got here in the first place. Your success has brought you isolation. When you get to the office each morning, you close your office door and hope nobody disturbs you. Any time you think to reach out to clients proactively, you quickly tell yourself you're too busy to pick up the phone or shoot out a quick email. In truth, you're avoiding what you might hear in reply.

"You need more than a new vision or dream. You need a way to share how you're feeling, get feedback on your ideas, and gain a greater sense of accountability. You need a feedback loop that will help you bring your new vison to life.

"Your picture of future success cannot simply live between your ears. You need advocates who care about you, your success, and the difference you want to make in the world. Believers who will help you stay on track."

But how could she find advocates like that? After years of pushing everyone away, how could she even start building connections again? Feeling overwhelmed and very alone, Nuria shut off the lights and went home. It was going to be a restless night.

CHAPTER 2

# DISCOVERING OVERREACH

## GRANT'S AWAKENING

**GRANT LOVED** the financial planning business. He took great pride in the difference he was making in the lives of his clients. He felt like a true partner to each client as he helped them achieve their most important personal and financial goals.

Now, he wondered if he had taken this idea of a partnership too far. In forming a client advisory board, he had hoped to pull together a group of clients who would support his ideas for expanding his practice and serving even more people. But he was quickly learning that they didn't always agree with him.

In retrospect, Grant realized he had probably been hoping for a group of people who would rubber-stamp everything that he suggested. After all, they weren't in his industry, and they didn't understand the intricacies of investments and financial planning. That's why they'd hired him to be their financial planner in the first place.

But his clients—very successful business owners, executives, and retirees—took their advisory responsibilities very seriously. They felt compelled to tell it like they saw it. And sometimes that made Grant squirm in his seat.

Now, getting ready to pitch them his next can't-miss idea, Grant took a deep breath and tried to control his emotions.

"Please, just hear me out," he pleaded. "I know that the last few initiatives haven't performed as well as I hoped, but this one is different. My new ad campaign will blow people's minds. It's edgy, it's provocative, and it's going to get people talking about New Wave Financial like they never have before. My company's name will be on the lips of everybody in the region who needs an elite financial planner like me. My phone will be ringing off the hook."

The board members looked at each other skeptically. They had heard wild claims like this from Grant before.

"What proof do you have that it will work?" one of them asked. "Or rather, that it'll work well enough to justify the huge budget you're asking for?"

"I've done my market research," Grant replied, pulling up a slide on his laptop. "I know that this campaign is going to resonate with our target audience. I'll dominate social media."

The board members looked skeptically at the slide.

"Think about it, Grant," another advisory board member jumped in. "Your success has been a result of the strong referral network you've built. It hasn't required expensive ad campaigns. You told us that you already have limited time to meet with prospective clients, so even if you're right and the campaign works, you won't have time to keep up with all the folks who'll suddenly be reaching out to you for help."

"Plus," yet another board member chimed in, "you told us about the new regulations that will be coming down the pike from Washington next month. You said they could throw a major kink in your operations. You'll be reworking systems and retraining your team members. Is now really the right time to add more to your plate?"

Grant nodded, feeling deflated, and said he would follow their advice. He knew they were right, but he couldn't shake the feeling that he was missing out on an important opportunity.

As he left the board meeting, his inner voice began to speak.

"You don't have to give up on your idea completely," it said. "You just need to find a way to make it work within the priorities you've set for your business. Maybe you should start small and build momentum from there."

Grant considered this and felt a glimmer of hope. He returned to his office and started brainstorming, determined to find a way to achieve his goals while staying focused on his priorities.

He had to admit that he tended to get too hung up on big, complicated ideas. He wanted to swing for the fences every time he came to the plate. But deep down he knew that the success he had achieved so far had come by hitting singles and doubles.

He wished he had the right kind of support—a mentor or friend reminding him to start small every time he got carried away. His board was great, but what he really needed was someone he could bounce ideas off of, in a lower-stakes setting than a board room. But where to find peers who would listen to him? He'd need to keep thinking.

CHAPTER 3

# CONFRONTING WORKAHOLISM

## BO'S AWAKENING

**FOR THE THIRD TIME** this week, Bo found himself staying late at the office, struggling to answer a seemingly endless barrage of emails while also pulling together a lead sheet he'd promised to a client by end-of-day. He had started the day with the best intentions, but by 4 p.m., he was scrambling just to keep up with the flood of incoming requests, let alone finish his most important project. At 8 p.m., he finally packed up and headed home. As he locked the doors at Top Strategy Marketing, he wondered how he could continue this hamster wheel routine. First to arrive, last to leave, and no time for lunch most days. That's certainly not how he'd pictured the life of a successful business owner when he opened TSM.

When Bo arrived at home, his wife, Maddie, reheated his dinner without even asking him if he was hungry. In fact, she didn't even say hello. They were both on autopilot, going through the motions of a marriage that had taken a back seat to the overwhelming busyness at TSM. Bo couldn't even remember the last time his family had all had a relaxing meal together.

Just as he took his first bite, Bo's son, Dudley, ran excitedly into the room. "Only two more wins and we'll be in the playoffs," he exclaimed as he plopped down on a chair next to his dad.

Bo instantly set down his fork, appetite draining away even after a long day with only a pack of cheese crackers and a diet soda for nourishment. He had done it again—completely forgotten about his son's baseball game. Years ago, Bo had been the one to throw Dudley his first pitch, convinced they would enjoy baseball as a father and son duo. He even coached Dudley's team for a few years. Now he couldn't even make it to a single game. How could he be a good dad when he was always buried in his work?

"That's great about the playoffs," he said to Dudley, working to keep his voice cheerful. His guilt wasn't his son's problem. Before Dudley could say anything else, his sister, Janey, shouted from the family room, "Hurry up, Dudley! Our favorite show is about to start."

Bo smiled at Dudley and gave him a wink, letting him know it was okay to go into the other room and watch TV.

"He got three hits today. It would've meant a lot to him to see you at the game," Maddie said quietly. "I hope you're proud of yourself."

Bo picked up his fork and began to eat. Better to ignore her than to get into another argument, he thought. Maddie apparently felt the same way, as she left the room to watch the TV show with their kids. The hamster wheel kept spinning.

Just then, Bo's inner voice spoke up. "You need to get a grip on your time management. You're always putting work first and neglecting your family. You can't keep going like this. You'll end up losing the people you hold most dear."

Bo nodded to himself, realizing his inner voice was right. He needed to find a better way to balance his work and family life. But he couldn't recall how many times he had talked about balance with Maddie, gotten home on time for a few days in a row, and then upset the apple cart with yet another late night at the office.

He wondered if this time would be any different.

He knew it wouldn't. He needed to make some radical changes. Though his family was most important, he also realized that the long hours he was regularly putting in did not equate to success at work. Most of his time was spent putting out fires, not concentrating on the projects that were important to his clients and his team.

Plus, his work felt empty. He no longer had the fire in his belly that had helped him get TSM off the ground. The purpose and impact that had guided so much early success had turned into a distant memory.

As he put his dinner plate in the dishwasher, he didn't even want to think about the extra inches surrounding his waistline. His health routines had fallen victim to his poor time management too. He knew his constant grinding was eventually going to cause serious health problems. And without good health, he would be no good at home or at work.

Heading to the den to return emails he hadn't gotten to at the office, Bo passed the family room where his wife and kids were giggling together in front of the TV. They seemed so happy, he thought. They didn't even seem to know he was missing.

CHAPTER 4

# ENTER TITO

## OUR HEROES SET OFF ON A JOURNEY

**NURIA, GRANT, AND BO** had been friends for a few years. They had initially connected through a monthly business networking group called Movers and Shakers. Eventually deciding these events weren't really leading to new business opportunities, they'd decided instead to meet every month or so for breakfast. Their time together, though admittedly just as unproductive as the networking events, was always enjoyable. They all loved to gossip about what was going on around town, as well as indulge in serious debate about the local sports teams.

Gathering at their favorite breakfast spot, Tito's Diner, for the first time in seven weeks, the usually energetic trio all looked like they needed a few more hours of sleep.

"Black coffee served intravenously," Bo joked to the waitress as he arrived at the table ten minutes late. Bo was always the last to get there.

"Did you have a late night?" Nuria asked.

"Not really. I just didn't sleep very well."

"Me either," Grant offered.

"Me three," Nuria agreed.

"My, aren't we just a bowl of sunshine this morning?" Bo

remarked. "Maybe we should order pillows and blankets instead of breakfast."

"Seriously, what made you two restless last night?" Nuria asked.

"I couldn't get my mind to stop thinking about my business," Grant answered.

"Ditto that," Bo said.

"Once again, me three," Nuria offered. "I was thinking about what life would be like if I sold my business and found something else to do. I just lost a big client, and it made me realize how out of kilter things are at Custom Design Group. And that's impacting things at home too. There's not much joy going around. Just grind, grind, grind, and I still feel behind."

"Whoa," Bo jumped in, "welcome to my world. If I don't get control over the way I'm spending my time, I might lose my business, my family, and my life. I know that sounds dramatic, but I spent most of the night thinking about how much of a workaholic I've become. I dreamed I was strapped to a ticking time bomb."

"Can I join the pity party?" Grant asked. "I'm stuck in a trap of always trying to bite off more than I can chew. My mind constantly drifts into thoughts about grand new projects and bright, shiny plans that will revolutionize my business. If they could, I think my client advisory board would fire me."

"You know," Bo said, "we sound like a bunch of spoiled kids. We have successful businesses. We have families who love us. We're making a difference in the community. Now we want more. We want to move to new levels of success. But change is hard. The things that got us to where we are today won't get us to where we want to go next."

"You're right," said Nuria. "And this is the first time in a long while that our breakfast conversation has been about our lives and our businesses. We usually just gossip and talk about sports."

"No doubt about it," Bo answered. "Don't get me wrong, I value our friendships and just chatting with you two, but I'm starting to think we could be more than friends to each other. We could also be mentors and accountability partners. Between the three of us, I bet we could solve the challenges we've been losing so much sleep over."

"I don't know," Grant said. "We do have the brainpower, but I think we need more than that. We need a system or a process or something to make sure we don't just spin our wheels. If this is something we're serious about, we need to turn ideas into actions so we can measure our results."

"That sounds like something a financial planner would say," Bo joked.

"Very funny, Bo," Grant shot back. "Thankfully you're sitting with the best financial planner in town, if I do say so myself."

"It's getting late," said Nuria, "and as usual I have a lot of work to do. But how about instead of waiting another month, we meet back here in a week and talk more about this accountability partnership thing?"

The three left the diner together, tentatively hopeful about what was to come.

The following Friday morning, Grant arrived first at Tito's Diner and claimed his favorite booth. He'd worked on more projects than he could count at this table over the years. A bottomless cup of coffee, a good Wi-Fi connection, and this quiet table made for a great sanctuary when he wanted to be away from his office.

Today, he felt it would be a perfect location for brainstorming with Nuria and Bo.

"Let's get down to business," he started. "I was thinking we should begin with each of us sharing what we want out of an accountability partner or mentoring connection. I'm guessing we all have different perspectives."

Bo offered to go first. "I learn best when I have a chance to interact with others who are also open to sharing, listening, and offering and receiving feedback. I don't need to constantly hear myself talk, and I don't like being around folks who do."

Nuria was next to share. "We need to have structure. We can't just sit down, start talking, and hope to get something done. Each meeting should have an agenda on which we all agree."

When it was Grant's turn, he suggested, "We should help each other set goals, or at least clearly understand each other's most important priorities. That way we can hold each other accountable. Ideally, our group will help each of us think strategically, put ideas into action, and review results."

"We're onto something here," Bo offered enthusiastically. "We each seem to need invisible partners in our businesses—other people who know enough about what we're trying to accomplish to help keep us pointed in the right direction. We each know that sometimes that means talking and sometimes it means listening. Sometimes we need to be the student and other times we need to be the teacher. And it's not going to happen by chance. We need to approach our time together with intentionality."

Just then, bearing an armload of breakfast plates, Tito, the diner's owner, unexpectedly joined the conversation: "You need a roundtable."

"No," Bo joked, "this booth is just fine."

"That's not what I meant," Tito shot back, "and I think you know it. What I just heard you describing is a business roundtable. It's one of the secrets to any successful endeavor. Groups like yours come into my restaurant all the time. They have all these fancy ideas about giving each other referrals or being masters of the universe. But what they're really looking for is a cohort of like-minded people who understand that the best way to get is to give. The best way to grow and learn is to be willing to share, mentor, and teach."

"Sounds like you have some experience with roundtables," Grant said. "Do you have time to tell us more?"

"Not right now," Tito answered, "but get started on your breakfast and I'll come back in about ten minutes."

The trio quickly began to recall what they knew about Tito. After all, most business gurus don't wear aprons and serve coffee in a diner early in the morning, even when they own one of the best restaurants in town.

Tito was a local legend. He was born and raised in the area and gained a great deal of recognition as a high school baseball star. He then went across the state to play at the university, where he became the best first baseman in the country. After graduating, he was drafted by the Cleveland Indians, the favorite major league baseball team of most local sports fans.

Unfortunately, his baseball career was cut short by injury and Tito seemed to disappear for about ten years. Most folks didn't know where he ended up until the local paper wrote a story about Tito's impending return to town with plans of opening a diner. The article said he had been living in Cleveland, where he had built a sizable investment management firm that he'd sold for an undisclosed fortune.

When asked why he was returning to his hometown to open a diner, he said he loved growing up in the area and always imagined himself coming home to raise his family and be part of the local business community. He had decided on a diner because he loved to cook and had a little restaurant experience through a couple of his old firm's investments.

Tito's Diner had now been open for a handful of years. On the weekends, the line of folks waiting for pancakes wrapped around the building. Tito's success was evident, and once again Tito had gained a following of local admirers.

"This is really strange," Nuria remarked. "We came here to brainstorm and now we're getting ready to take advice from our waiter."

"Hold on," Grant interrupted. "Tito isn't just any old waiter. I know a lot about his old investment firm because we use some of their mutual funds in the portfolios we manage for our financial planning clients. He's literally a business genius."

"Yeah, I don't know all the details," Bo continued, "but I've heard that he likes to keep a low profile. He doesn't want to be in the headlines anymore. He just wants to make his diner as good as it can be."

Grant added, "A lot of important people still come to him for investment advice, and he helps them out, but that's not his focus anymore. He says this diner is his pride and joy. He really loves this place and all his customers. That's why he's around all the time."

"Sounds like he's a bit eccentric," Nuria suggested.

"Maybe,'" Grant replied, "but I'm guessing having this eccentric waiter point us in the right direction could really be a stroke of fate."

"I totally agree," Bo said. "Let's hear what he has to say."

As promised, Tito came back to the table ten minutes later. He was armed with a fresh pot of coffee, a small plate of bacon, and a thick envelope that said "Dream Big" on the front.

"I brought some extra nourishment," he said. "I like to think of it as brain food."

They all nodded in agreement as they each filled their mugs and snagged a slice of bacon.

"Sorry if I seemed rude jumping into your conversation earlier," Tito began, "but, as you can imagine, I hear bits and pieces of many conversations during the breakfast rush. And I notice the folks who gather with the purpose of networking or building their businesses. It's usually well-intended. But too often, what starts with a purpose winds up with nothing happening. Meaningful conversations end up in chatter about last night's game or what's in store for the weekend. Don't get me wrong; that's okay. After all, they're still buying breakfast. But nothing makes me happier than to see folks like you turn a simple breakfast meeting into something more meaningful."

"As you correctly guessed, that's why we're here," Grant offered. "We're not sure exactly what we're after, but we know we want to find a way to help each other grow, personally and professionally."

"Good on you," Tito encouraged. "I'd like to help. I'm good at helping folks bring out the best in themselves. Partly because my own roundtable has helped me build my business into the most successful restaurant in town—excuse the bragging. And partly because my role in running this place has put me in a position to offer lots of advice. Like now. Even when you didn't ask for it."

"I know you owned and sold a very successful investment firm," Grant offered. "Did you have a roundtable back then?"

"Not at first," Tito answered, "but I had the good fortune of meeting some incredible Truest Fans through my business, and they eventually led to me becoming part of a roundtable. Being the Truest Fan has been part of my life for a long time."

Nobody knew yet what a Truest Fan was, but they liked the sound of it. It resonated with what all their inner voices had been saying lately—that they needed to invest in their own work and the people around them in a new way.

"How does your roundtable work?" Bo asked.

"We meet here at 5:00 a.m. every Tuesday," Tito answered. "Given my current profession, we start extra early. Right now there are five of us, but our group started out with just three and we've had as many as seven. I've found that groups in that size range can get a lot done in sixty minutes. No one in our group likes long meetings. And we always have an agenda that's based on the Truest Fan Blueprint."

"What's the Truest Fan Blueprint?" Grant questioned.

Tito replied, "It's our roadmap for staying on course. Like any of the great models you may have studied for personal and professional development, it provides a guiding light for exploring, defining, and implementing new ideas. We'd be lost without it."

"How come I've never heard about it before?" Bo inquired.

Tito answered, "I honestly don't know. It's not a secret. In fact, do you see that big table under the window? That's the meeting spot for a Truest Fan Roundtable that's been gathering here for years. And I bet you've done business with some of them. They run what we call Truest Fan businesses. Through their businesses and their interactions in the community, they have all committed to living, loving, serving, and leading with purpose and impact. They don't just want to make money; they want to make a real difference in the world."

"That sounds kind of high-minded to me," Grant shot back. "The idea of a Truest Fan feels a bit woo-woo."

"Not at all, not at all," Tito argued. "In fact, the idea of a Truest Fan goes back to one of the oldest lessons in the world—the idea that we should all treat each other the way we would like to be treated ourselves. When you're someone's Truest Fan, you look for ways to offer them encouragement and cheer them on. We want to be the Truest Fans of our family, friends, clients, customers—in fact, anyone we encounter in life. But especially when you're in a roundtable together, you use all that positive energy to create change together."

"I never really thought about things that way before," Bo said, "but it makes perfect sense. So how does it work in the roundtables? Do you have a set of rules that you use?"

"More guideline than rules," Tito answered. "We have a specific structure. I can teach it to you if you want."

"By the way, how do you know that other group is a Truest Fan Roundtable?" Bo asked.

"Funny you ask," Tito replied. "I helped start that group by doing exactly what I'm doing with you all today. I noticed they needed help. Like today, I kind of inserted myself into the conversation and explained all about the Truest Fan Blueprint and how to use it to form a roundtable. They jumped in headfirst, and they've been meeting here ever since. For a while, I sat in their meetings and helped them get things started, but now they pretty much run things on their own."

Nuria, the apparent taskmaster in the group, jumped in. "Okay, this sounds like it could be really helpful. What do you suggest we do next?"

Before Tito could answer, Bo chimed in. "I think we should start a Truest Fan Roundtable of our own. What Tito has described is exactly what we were talking about earlier. Why should we reinvent the wheel? Let's just try his model and see how it works."

"I don't have an objection," Nuria replied. "I'm just an analytical type and this seems almost too easy."

"Hold on," Tito said, "the principles of the Truest Fan Roundtable are simple, but they are not easy. The work doesn't all happen during the roundtable; it mostly happens when the members of the roundtable take what they've been given and put it into action in their businesses and lives. And sometimes that's hard. The Truest Fans I have encountered are some of the hardest-working folks I know. They're not afraid to work hard, because they have the confidence of knowing that they're working on ideas that are pointing them toward achieving their biggest dreams."

"What do you mean by big dreams?" Grant asked.

"That's a great question," Tito answered. "In fact, it's the first step in the Truest Fan Blueprint. If you really want to move forward in creating a Truest Fan Roundtable, that would be the first assignment I would give you."

"You want to give us an assignment?" Nuria asked.

"Well, they say when the student is ready, the teacher appears," Tito joked. "Seems my showing up at your booth today is just what you needed."

The trio simultaneously nodded their heads in agreement.

"Excellent," Tito said. "Before I get into teacher mode, though, I would first like to set a simple ground rule. I'm willing to get you started. I'll give you some assignments and I'll sit in on your first meetings. I'll make sure you're heading in the right direction. But the sooner you can take what you learn and do it on your own, the better. After all, this is your roundtable, not mine."

"That sounds fair," Grant answered.

CHAPTER 5

# DREAM BIG

**"ALL RIGHT THEN,"** Tito said, "your first assignment is to record your biggest dreams. I want you to take some time to think about what your life will be like ten years from now. Put your imagination on full throttle. What will things look like in your business? What will things look like in your personal life? Who will be around you? What accomplishments will you have achieved? They should be both personal dreams and professional dreams. There are absolutely no limitations.

"I have found that the best way to conduct this exercise is to go into a quiet space, turn off all your devices and distractions, get out a blank sheet of paper and simply start writing. Don't create unnecessary rules. Always remember that these are your dreams and nobody else's, so there are no wrong answers. Don't hold back. Dream as big and as boldly as you can.

"Think of it like writing your future biography. Make it a grand story full of excitement, joy, and adventure, not a dull journal nobody would ever want to read. Write a story you'll want to live and retell over and over again.

"A few days after your first Dream Big session, sit down again, no distractions, and dream some more. Don't try to edit what you wrote previously, just add and expand on it. Remember that one of the keys to success is to be able to picture yourself succeeding. The more vividly you picture your future successes and revisit your big dreams, the more likely they are to come true.

"That's why it's so important to spend time on this. As you begin to form more specific plans around the things you want to accomplish in shorter periods of time, you'll be able to measure them against your big dreams. You'll be surer that the things you're doing today will help you fulfill the dreams that you have for tomorrow. When I see you next time, we'll talk about your big dreams, and you'll share them with each other. Then we'll talk about the next step on your Truest Fan journey."

"Well," Grant said, "that actually sounds fun. I love to dream and think about the future. Although I must admit that sometimes I cut myself off from dreaming because I start to feel nervous that my dreams are well beyond what's possible. And I'm famous for trying to bite off more than I can chew. Just ask my client advisory board."

"A lot of people do that," Tito replied.

"I see it completely differently," Nuria interjected. "I think this exercise sounds terrifying. I know I need a new vison for my business and my life. But I don't really like to dream about what the future may look like. Maybe it's because my mom always used to try to keep me on track and tell me not to daydream. But we agreed to give this a try, so I'm going to complete this assignment, even if I think it might be difficult."

"That's great," Tito replied. "How about you, Bo?"

"I guess I'm somewhere in the middle," Bo answered. "I'm not a big dreamer—or at least, I never write my dreams down.

But I'm not afraid of dreaming. As we said, let's just give this a try and see what happens."

"I can promise you one thing," Tito said. "If you take what we're talking about seriously, you'll grow immeasurably. I can't wait to hear about your big dreams next week."

They all agreed to Dream Big in the coming week and to meet at the diner again in a week's time.

"One more thing," Tito continued as he opened the envelope on his tray with the words "Dream Big" on the front, he had brought with him. "I got this envelope out of my office when I picked up the coffee and bacon. I'd like you each to use one of these cards to complete the Dream Big exercise; it will remind you what this assignment's all about."

The card's heading read, "Dream Big." In the middle was empty space designated for completing the exercise. Toward the bottom, the phrase "Don't hold back" was written for encouragement. Finally, the Truest Fan vision statement appeared: "We live to love, to serve, and to lead others with purpose and impact."

## DREAM BIG

## DON'T HOLD BACK

*WE LIVE TO LOVE, TO SERVE, AND TO LEAD OTHERS WITH PURPOSE AND IMPACT.*

CHAPTER 6

# NURIA STRUGGLES TO DREAM BIG

**THE FOLLOWING DAY,** Nuria arrived at her office early, determined not to procrastinate on her Dream Big exercise. Despite feeling intimidated about capturing her dreams, she prided herself on following through with her commitments. However, as she stared at her Dream Big card, she was hit with a severe case of writer's block. Although she yearned to explore possibilities beyond her current work, her mind was blank. Then she remembered the sleepless night she had the past week. She had contemplated selling her business and starting all over again. But that didn't feel like a dream; it felt like giving up something that worked, even if she didn't always enjoy it. It felt like quitting. This led to feelings of frustration and hopelessness, causing her to jot down a few notes and to decide to come back to the exercise in a couple of days, as Tito had advised.

When Nuria returned to the Dream Big exercise, she began to doubt the effectiveness of staring at a piece of paper to achieve her goals. Her thoughts kept running into dead ends. However, a mental image of at-risk children suddenly came to mind, reminding her of her desire to serve causes that would enhance the lives of children who had faced similar struggles to what she had faced.

She wondered how these dreams aligned with her current path, feeling guilty in a way similar to how she felt when her mother told her to quit daydreaming. She feared she would have nothing useful to contribute when the group reconvened to review their Dream Big exercises.

CHAPTER 7

# OUR HEROES SHARE THEIR BIG DREAMS

**GRANT AND BO** arrived early for the next week's gathering, admitting they were excited to hear how things had gone for each other. Unusually, Nuria was the last to arrive, and she wasn't wearing her usual smile.

A few minutes later, Tito walked up to the table and asked, "How did it go? Did you finish the Dream Big exercise?"

They all nodded in unison.

Grant added, "We just compared notes and decided that the experience was different for each of us."

Tito chuckled. "That's the way it usually turns out. Dreaming big isn't as easy as it may sound. But I'm happy you each did what you committed to do. That's a big part of a successful Truest Fan Roundtable; you need to finish what you start. I'll be your waiter today," he added. "What are you having for breakfast?"

Excited to get into the day's business, they each quickly agreed on Tito's daily special.

"That was fast," Tito remarked. "Now I want you to take one more step in thinking about your big dreams before we all sit down together." He went on to explain, "All of your big dreams are important, but most likely some of them stand out to you more than others. When you read them out loud or think about them, they spark some added excitement. In many cases you may be able to visualize yourself in those dreams. You can actually see yourself accomplishing them. Maybe you picture the scenery or the people around you or the recognition you receive. What I'd like you to do is choose the three dreams that stand out the most. You can just circle them on your paper. After you've chosen your top three dreams, I want you to put a star next to the one that stands out the most."

"That doesn't seem fair," Bo exclaimed. "I'm excited about all my dreams."

"I'm sure you are, Bo," Tito replied, "but for now I just want you to focus on the top three and then the single most important one. You'll understand why when we get back together to talk about them."

At that point, Tito went off to get their breakfast while Grant, Nuria, and Bo began to prioritize. They didn't say a word to each other; they were totally lost in their dreams.

As Tito returned to the table with their food about ten minutes later, he noticed that Bo and Grant had finished the exercise, while Nuria seemed to need more time. She stared at the page with her head in her hand, tapping her pen softly on the table.

"Pens down—your time is up," Tito joked.

Nuria extended her index finger in the classic one-more-minute pose.

"Take as much time as you need, Nuria," Tito offered. "This isn't a test. I've always wanted to say that."

Just then, Nuria looked up and said, "I'm finished. And by the way, I was always the last one to finish my exams, so I'm used to those instructions."

They all laughed.

As Tito placed their plates in front of them, he told them that the next step in the exercise was for each one of them to share their biggest dream, the one dream they had highlighted, the one that stood out above the rest.

Bo was anxious to go first.

"This might sound silly," he began. "I picture the name of my company, Top Strategy Marketing, at the top of a high-rise office tower in the middle of downtown, overlooking the river. My team's offices will be on the top floor, and that represents the financial success of my business. We'll also have a floor dedicated as an incubator for business startups as my way of giving back to the business community. And we'll have a rent-free floor as office space for local nonprofit organizations. I see my success and the success of my business as a way not only to provide for me, my family, and my team, but also as a way to help others, whether they're starting their own businesses or serving important needs in our community."

"Wow," Grant exclaimed, "that's really impressive!"

"Maybe," Bo answered. "I have to admit, our discussion about what it means to be a Truest Fan impacted my biggest dream, even though I didn't set out to think about it that way. I want to be successful, but I also want to use my good fortune to help others."

"Okay, who's next?" Tito asked.

"I'll go," Grant answered, "although I don't think my big dream is nearly as amazing as what Bo just shared."

"Hold on," Tito broke in. "Remember what I said last week. These are *your* big dreams. It's not a competition. Don't try to compare yourself to anybody else; comparison is the thief of joy."

"Sorry, Tito," Grant apologized. "Phase one of my big dream is to have one hundred of my ideal clients, each with a minimum of one million dollars that my team and I manage. With my current fee schedule that would mean I would have a business that generated over one million dollars in annually recurring revenues. In all likelihood, my revenues would be much greater, but I like round numbers. With these one hundred clients I would know that I had the business I've always hoped for, working with people that I really enjoy and can serve the best. It would also put me in a position to comfortably support my family, and I would be able to financially support the causes that I care about. The way I see it, winning in my business and serving these clients would lead to greater fulfillment in all aspects of my life."

"That's great," Tito said. "You have a big dream that emanates from your business and impacts all the important aspects of your life. Well done. But you said that was phase one. Is there a phase two?"

"Yes, there is. Phase two will include creating a network of other advisors who would like to build their practices the same way I'll have built my own. I'm still dreaming about what that may look like."

"Excellent," Tito approved. "If you keep following the Truest Fan model, you'll have time to keep dreaming. Who's next?"

"Well," Nuria hesitated, "I guess that's me. I have to admit, this is a little nerve-racking. It was hard enough for me to go through this exercise by myself, and now I have to share it with other people?"

"No worries," Bo said. "We're all in this together."

Nuria continued, "My big dream is to be in a position to sell my business for a handsome profit so that I can start a nonprofit organization that offers support to at-risk children. I'm still trying to picture exactly what the nonprofit will do, but I know it has something to do with kids. As much as I love my current business, it's not helping the causes I care about very directly. So I can picture getting my business to a point where it can run without me. Then I'll be able to sell it to somebody who's ready to take it to the next level. Someone who can carry on my business legacy. I'd love that to be one or more of my long-term teammates. Does that make sense?"

"Absolutely," Grant jumped in. "I love it. And I've seen you around children; you're great with them. With your big dream you'll have an even bigger impact."

"These are all great big dreams," Tito said. "You've absolutely taken the first step toward becoming Truest Fans and building your Truest Fan Roundtable. You each have dreams you've been able to articulate to each other. By saying your dreams out loud, you're accomplishing two things. First, you can see that the goal of your roundtable is more than just supporting each other in conducting your day-to-day business. You're actually supporting worthwhile causes that could impact tens of thousands of people. You'll take your work here more seriously when you know what it's for. Second, articulating your big dreams is like creating a huge magnet that's going to pull you forward into the future. You can use these dreams to measure each of the goals and priorities that you make along the way. You can ask yourself, 'Is this thing going to help me get closer to my big dream?' If it does, you can say yes and move forward. If it doesn't, it gives you an opportunity to say no and avoid those things that aren't actually important."

"Hold on," Nuria said somewhat sternly. "You're making this sound way too easy. Remember, when we met a couple weeks ago, we'd all had trouble sleeping the night before."

"Yes, I remember," Grant replied.

"Well," said Nuria, "I couldn't sleep before because my vision for the future was an absolute wreck. I knew I needed to dream, to cast a new vision, but I had run into a brick wall. And sure, I've shared a clean new picture of what my future may look like, but coming to this point was really hard."

"Keep going," Tito encouraged.

"I lost a ton more sleep over the past week," she continued. "Trying to articulate my dreams forced me to face some stuff I'd been hiding from."

"That sounds tough," Grant sympathized. "What kind of stuff?"

Nuria shrugged, gazing down at her pancakes. "The truth is, I'm terribly lonely. I've always been a loner. My greatest companion growing up was my computer. I loved writing code and building websites. So when it came to starting a career, web design seemed like a natural thing to do. I could hide behind my giant computer screens. When I decided to go out on my own to build my company, it wasn't because of some entrepreneurial itch. My former company had gotten too big, and I didn't like working around so many people. I just wanted something small that I could control.

"For me, finding the right number of team members came easy. Not because I was good with people, but because I know systems and processes. I viewed building a business like solving a puzzle. I just had to put the right pieces in place, and keep it as small as possible.

"Fortunately, one of my clients from my former company really liked my work and we were able to continue working together. She was also a great networker, so she loved introducing me to other business owners. I never really had to go looking for clients. They came to me through my initial client and then through other introductions from subsequent clients. I didn't even have to ask. Who knows how things would have turned out if I had actually had to sell myself and my company?

"Don't get me wrong. We're doing some amazing work. Our customers love us—at least most of them do. We've helped them achieve their visons and dreams. But my success hasn't really come from some grand vison. I started my business because I was running away from something, not running toward a dream. I wanted to fight feelings of loneliness by controlling my environment.

"Nowadays, I stay cooped up in my office reacting to my team and my clients through text messages and emails. In many ways, my computer is still my best friend. What's worse, sometimes that's the way I communicate with my husband and kids. And I think that's why I've had on-and-off thoughts about selling my business. I'm getting the same feeling I had when I left my last company. The bigger we grow, the more isolated and uncomfortable I feel. I wonder how I can be so lonely when there are so many people around me who want to be part of my success.

"I'm hiding and shrinking back even though I really want to make a difference in the world. I want the best for my family, team, and clients. Plus I want to help children who may be going through some of the same stuff I've experienced."

She cut off, still not making eye contact with anyone, playing with her fork instead. Everyone was silent for a moment, absorbing all that Nuria had shared.

"Thanks for being so honest and vulnerable with us," Grant offered finally. "Based on the way you carry yourself and the reputation of your company, I never would have guessed you had that kind of inner struggle."

"To tell you the truth, Grant," Nuria interjected, "until I went through the Dream Big exercise this past week, I didn't realize it myself. I had kept it bottled up."

"Besides coming up with your big dream, what did you learn?" Tito asked.

"I learned that I could use my past struggles as a source of inspiration for my future dreams. My past, especially the parts I like to bottle up inside me, doesn't define me. I can't be afraid of stepping outside of my comfort zone when pursuing my dreams."

"Bravo," Bo responded. "Thanks for trusting us with everything you've been thinking. It couldn't have been easy."

"Thanks for listening," Nuria offered. "It felt good to be able to say those things out loud. I've never done it before, but I'm hopeful our roundtable will give each of us a chance to be more open. That's going to be an important part of making it worthwhile."

"Definitely," Tito agreed.

"I'm still not totally clear on where this is all headed," Grant admitted. "But now I'm beginning to believe even more that we need to trust the process. We're going to discover a lot about ourselves. We'll dig out some hard truths. By bringing them into the light, we can find ways to overcome them."

"As you might have guessed, I was a bit skeptical about the assignment when you first gave it to us last week, Tito," Nuria said. "Now it makes perfect sense. There's something about taking ideas you have in your head and in your heart and writing them down and then saying them out loud that brings them to life."

"Great observation," Tito said. "You'll most likely achieve your big dreams even faster than you may have thought possible, because you have them so clearly in sight. A target is easier to hit when you can actually see it."

"Cheers to that," Bo exclaimed, punching his fist in the air. "I can't wait to get started."

"You have started," Tito countered. "By just picturing your big dreams, you've already placed yourselves on the path to achieve them. Every great adventure begins with a starting line. Think of today as your starting line."

CHAPTER 8

# THE 4D FRAMEWORK

**FOR THEIR NEXT ASSIGNMENT,** Tito said, "It's time to make time for the things that matter most."

"Sounds like magic," Bo joked. "I didn't know it was possible to make time."

"Actually," Tito shot back, "you can. Mostly by eliminating your distractions. You can't physically create more time, but you can decide how to better spend your time. Quite often that means developing systems for saying no to things that don't matter and yes to things that do."

"I think I understand what you're saying," Nuria said. "I'm constantly being bombarded with ideas and questions from clients and colleagues. I try to respond as quickly as I can, but I'm never able to keep up. At the end of the day, when I look back at what I've done, I feel like I've only done the things that other people asked me to do and not the things that I set out at the beginning of the day to do for myself."

"That's a great example," Tito said sympathetically. "When we don't have systems for deciding our priorities, we end up making other people's priorities our priorities. We let simple questions that come from our teams and from our clients turn into urgent, "must do now" activities because we feel we have to be responsive to our teammates or to our clients. Like we need to be at their beck and call. But when you stop to think about it, the inefficiencies these interruptions create make us less responsive to our teammates, and we probably end up giving worse service to our clients."

"I know that's true for me," Grant offered. "Sometimes a client says to me something like, 'Oh, thanks for getting this to me so soon, I wasn't expecting it for a couple of weeks.' At that point, I angrily think to myself, *I stopped doing other important things to get this project done and they didn't really need a rapid response.* That's frustrating, and it happens too often in the name of client service. I've done it with the people on my team too. I guess it's because I always want people to be happy, but maybe my definition of happiness takes it too far and causes other problems."

"That's part of it," Tito answered. "More generally, though, we prioritize those things that we like doing most, or maybe find easy to get done the fastest. Little things we can check off on our lists quickly. Think about your daily to-do lists. When you look at them at the end of a busy day, is the stuff that's left mostly the bigger, more important priorities? You know, the items that may take more time, thought, and energy? You make three or four or five small check marks that are less important even in combination than the big one you set out to accomplish at the start of the day."

"That's a dirty word," Bo laughed.

"What word?" Tito asked.

"To-do list," Bo shot back. "I can't tell you how many times I've tried to come up with new systems to manage my to-do list, and I never seem to get to the bottom of it. So 'to-do list' has become a dirty word for me. I like to pretend that I don't even have one."

They all laughed.

"I think we've all been there," Tito replied. "Just go into the bookstore and look at all the self-help books about prioritization, time management, and getting the most out of your day. If there was one simple answer, there wouldn't be so many different books. The good news is that the Truest Fan Blueprint contains a simple framework for taming your out-of-control to-do list and many of the other things that may be getting in your way. This week, I want you to give it a try."

Tito gave everyone oversized index cards, resembling the Dream Big cards they had received the previous week. The heading stated, "The 4D Framework for Eliminating Distractions." Near the bottom were the four Ds—"Delete, Delegate, Defer, Do"—followed by a reminder, "Spend your time working on the things that matter most." As before, the Truest Fan vision statement appeared at the very bottom: "We live to love, to serve, and to lead others with purpose and impact."

Tito explained, "The 4D Framework is all about uncovering the most important activities to focus on. This could be the most important tasks in the current day, the current month, or the current quarter. For now I want you to focus on each day. The best part is, if you get this right, you will literally find that you've gained hours back in your days. You'll almost immediately find that you have more time for some of the big things that you've been putting off. And you'll be working more toward your big dreams on a daily basis."

"Call me a skeptic," Bo said, "but I've heard this kind of promise before. How is this system different than what's on the pages of all those self-help books you were talking about?"

Tito grinned. "There's a naysayer in every crowd. And I must admit I take great pleasure in seeing them eat crow after giving the 4D Framework a test drive."

"Well," Bo replied, "I didn't know you served crow at Tito's Diner. It must be one of your specials."

"Now, now, boys," Nuria interrupted. "Enough of this bravado. If Tito says this 4D thing works, I'm more than willing to give it to a try."

"Please accept my apology," Tito said with a wry smile. "Now you have two choices. You can either apply the 4D Framework to your daily to-do list, or you can apply it to your email inbox. When you think about your typical day, where do you get more hung up? Keeping up with your emails? Or choosing which items on your to-do list you'll work on and putting them in order?"

"That's a tough one," Grant admitted. "I wrestle with both of them every day."

"Don't worry," Tito replied, "you'll eventually work on both. In fact, you'll probably uncover new ways to use the 4D Framework once you learn how to put it into action. It will be one of those tools that you'll come back to time and time again. First, set aside about fifteen minutes of planning time at the beginning of your day. During that time, you'll simply review each item on your list and decide whether to delete, delegate, defer, or do it that day."

"Wait a second," Bo objected. "Did you say set aside time to plan each day? Who has time for that? When I get to the office, I need to jump right in. I don't have any time for planning."

"I resemble that remark," Grant agreed.

"I sometimes feel that way too," Nuria concurred, "but I always find that the days I plan out are the days I get the most done."

"You're absolutely right, Nuria," Tito said. "A good day almost always begins with a good plan. The 4D Framework makes the planning more efficient and effective. Once you get used to it, it hardly takes any time at all. And by the way, Bo, this is probably why you struggle with all those other systems. Just about every system out there requires regular planning."

"Okay, okay," Bo said with exasperation. "I will give it a try, but I don't have to like it."

"That's all I ask," said Tito. "So when you're sitting with your to-do list during your planning time, first decide which tasks you can delete. Most of us put more things on our to-do lists than we ever intend or even need to do. Sometimes it's our way of trying not to let things slip through the cracks. Other times, the tasks we add to our lists during the day get done as we go along, so they're no longer to-dos. When I first started doing this exercise, I found myself eliminating almost half of the stuff that was on my list. I'm a notorious list maker. Someone gives me an idea; I write it down like they were giving me an instruction. So in those early days I would feel extremely relieved when I found myself deleting fifty percent or more of the tasks on my list. If that was all I had done, I would have gotten a great deal of time back. The other steps became icing on the cake."

"What if you delete something that you really needed to do?" Nuria asked.

"It makes total sense to worry about that, Nuria," Tito answered. "And I'm sure it happens, but I've also realized that those things that we really need to do always have a way of circling back around. When our minds are less cluttered because we don't have a long list, we think more clearly, and something that we may have crossed off our list will come back to us when we really need to do it. But there is rarely, if ever, anything that's life or death on a to-do list."

"Tell us about delegating," Grant encouraged. "I need to leave on time, I have another meeting right after our breakfast."

"Delegating is pretty much like it sounds," Tito continued. "After you've deleted the things that don't need to be done, you need to decide which things on your list should be done by somebody else. It could be a teammate, a vendor, or a strategic partner. Think about each task; are you the right person to do it? And don't make the mistake of thinking that just because you *can* do it, you *should*. Those people who support you have very important jobs and they're very good at doing the things that you have hired them to do. Give them the opportunity to succeed. Delegation builds leadership skills and creates greater teamwork. When the folks around you see that you trust them to do the things you're asking them to do, they'll begin to go out of their way to ask for even more. They will grow in their roles, and this will strengthen your team."

"I hear you," Bo replied, "but quite often I feel like I can get something done faster myself than teaching somebody else how to do it, or even giving the assignments."

"At times, I feel the same," Grant agreed, "even though I know it's a mistake. Like, my marketing assistant is smart and capable but she's not going to come up with the same ideas I am, so sometimes I end up doing her job for her—even though that makes her feel less valued and takes my time away from the financial research I'm supposed to be focused on."

"You'll get the hang of it," Tito encouraged. "In fact, let's make that officially part of your assignment this week, Grant; no matter what, let your marketing assistant do her job without interfering. The repetition of doing the 4D Framework every day will make you a better delegator. You'll get better at what you do and so will the people around you. In fact, you'll probably end up teaching your team the 4D Framework too.

"Now let's talk about defer," he continued. "Deferring is not procrastinating. Deferring is not putting off for the future the projects that are most difficult. But ask yourself, based on the nature of the task, if this is something that truly needs to be done today. If not, simply push it out on your calendar as a future task. Decide which day or week or month that task really needs to be done. I'm not suggesting you put things off to the last minute. Just remember, everything has its time and place. You can't do everything today.

"Finally, you'll have your new, shorter daily to-do list. Once you've deleted, delegated, and deferred, you'll have a handful of items left on your list. Those are the items that you need to block time off on your calendar to finish that day. Over time, I've found that I'm usually left with three to seven action items—for example, today I'm spending an hour with you three explaining the 4D method, I'm taking a three-hour shift waiting tables during the lunch rush, from two to four I'll handle this week's inventory management, and I've got a handful of phone calls to return. You notice how for the stuff that takes longer, I've planned specific blocks of time to get it done? I even dedicate a block of time for returning phone calls so I don't spend my day playing phone tag. I have a habit of leaving empty time blocks on my calendar each day to accomplish my biggest daily to-dos. I call this habit 'scheduling appointments with myself.' The way I figure it, I am one of the most important people in my own life. If I don't schedule time for myself the way that I do for my clients, employees, vendors, and my community activities, I'm cheating myself."

"And that's it?" Bo asked. "All the other stuff I've tried has been a lot more complicated, and that's probably why it hasn't worked for me. I like simple."

"Me too," Tito admitted, "and I think simplicity is at the heart of the 4D Framework. Are you ready to put it to work with your to-do lists?"

Bo and Grant quickly nodded in agreement, while Nuria had a question.

"I'm curious," she started, "you said that this method could also work as a way to manage an email inbox. That's a bigger pain point for me than my to-do list. How does that work?"

"Almost exactly the same way," Tito answered. "I suggest setting aside a dedicated time for responding to emails each day. For me, it's thirty minutes just after I finish my daily planning. I also have another shorter session, about fifteen minutes, after the lunch rush. During each of those email inbox sessions, I look at my inbox and decide what to delete, delegate, defer, or do.

"If you're like me, you get a lot of emails that you don't even need to pay attention to. Some are junk and some are just things that you're copied on for no good reason. Delete them. If you delete something important, it'll come back. Where appropriate, delegate emails that do not require your response. Defer the emails that don't require an immediate answer. And respond to the few emails that are left."

"Well," Nuria said, "I've made a rule for myself that I won't look at emails more than one time, so deferring would be really difficult."

"I totally get it," Tito responded, "but statistics show that the faster we respond to emails that don't require immediate attention, the more likely we are to get even more emails in return on the same subject. We like to feel we're being productive when we're sending all of those messages, when in truth we're just interrupting each other. Give it a try; hold off on responding to nonurgent emails just for a day or two. I'm sure you'll be glad that you did."

"I'll definitely give it a try," Nuria replied. "Anything will be better than what I'm doing right now."

"Well, good," Tito said. "It sounds like Bo and Grant are going to work on their to-do lists and Nuria is going to work on her email inbox using the 4D Framework this week. I promise, after just a day or two of doing this, you'll see how you start getting more done in less time just by making sure you're putting your most important daily priorities first."

"And saying no to a lot of other stuff," Bo added.

"I think you're going to be my best student this week," Tito offered. "Sometimes the doubters become the greatest students. Most importantly, have fun with this routine. Don't treat it like drudgery. You are mad scientists conducting experiments on yourselves and on the bad habits that are keeping you from having time for the things that you really want to do."

## THE 4D FRAMEWORK FOR ELIMINATING DISTRACTIONS

**DELETE, DELEGATE, DEFER, DO**

SPEND YOUR TIME WORKING ON THE THINGS THAT MATTER MOST. *WE LIVE TO LOVE, TO SERVE, AND TO LEAD OTHERS WITH PURPOSE AND IMPACT.*

CHAPTER 9

# BO BATTLES THE 4D FRAMEWORK

**AS BO LEFT THE MEETING,** he couldn't believe some of the words that had come out of his mouth. He had made it sound like he was really excited about the 4D Framework, but in truth he was scared to death. He knew that this was exactly the kind of thing that had gotten him into so much trouble in the past. He would get excited about a great idea, and then quickly blow it up by not following through on what he promised to do.

Based on the discussion they just had at breakfast, despite all his bravado, he figured there was a better chance he was going to let the group down than to actually be able to report back having had success. That also got him to thinking about the inner struggle he was having because of his workaholic tendencies and the fact that the way he was going was potentially going to ruin both his business and his family life.

The next morning, Bo pulled out his 4D Framework card and started to plan his day. Unfortunately, after spending more than an hour trying to decide what to delete and delegate, he was more confused than when he started. Deleting was difficult because he didn't know how to say no. He was a people pleaser, so if a colleague or a client asked him to do something, he simply added it to his list.

Delegating was similarly stressful because he didn't want to overload anyone else on his team. He preferred to sacrifice his own time than give a task to a teammate that might cause them to work late. His struggles with deleting and delegating meant he couldn't really consider how to defer or do. He went on with his day in his usual fashion, determined to try the 4D Framework again the following day.

And that's when things got worse. Bo was so preoccupied with that morning's 4D failure that he tried to overcompensate and get stuff off his to-do list by working until midnight. When he got home, the note on the kitchen counter read, "Dad, We lost the big game today. I really wish you could have been there. Our season is over. I needed you. Dudley." Maddie, his wife, had added a PS: "When will you learn? I can't do this alone."

Early the next morning, Bo left the house before anyone else was awake. He hadn't slept more than an hour and he didn't feel he could face Dudley or Maddie.

As Bo sat down to plan out his day, he felt a sense of determination wash over him. He knew that if he was going to turn his life around and be there for his family, he needed to start taking control of his time. He pulled out his 4D Framework card and decided to use it to its fullest potential. He began by deleting all the unnecessary tasks from his to-do list, including check-in phone calls and status meetings that didn't require his immediate attention. He then carefully assigned ongoing projects to his team, selecting the best person for the job based on their strengths and capabilities.

Bo felt a sense of satisfaction as he looked at his newly streamlined to-do list. He had removed all the clutter and was left with only the most important tasks that required his attention. He was confident that this would be the beginning of a new era, one where he could prioritize his time and focus on the things that truly mattered.

But as the day wore on, Bo's confidence began to wane. His team knew that he had a tendency to be a pushover, and they took advantage of his kindness by pulling him into meetings and tasks that weren't on his list. Bo found himself once again at the mercy of his schedule, feeling like he was being pulled in a million different directions. He knew he needed to be stronger and more assertive, but old habits die hard.

As the day drew to a close, Bo couldn't help but feel disappointed in himself. He had tried so hard to use the 4D Framework to his advantage, but he still found himself falling into old patterns of behavior. He knew that change wouldn't come overnight, but he couldn't help but wonder whether he was capable of making the necessary changes to turn his life around.

Deep down, Bo wanted nothing more than to be the teacher's pet when it came to the 4D Framework. He wanted to succeed more than anything else, but he also knew that his self-doubt and fear of failure were holding him back. He resolved to try again the next day, hoping that he could find the strength and courage to take control of his time and his life.

CHAPTER 10

# OUR HEROES LEARN HOW TO WIN THEIR BATTLES WITH TIME

**THE NEXT WEEK,** with Nuria, Grant, and Bo once again seated in their regular booth, the conversation was lively. They all had stories about the ways things had changed during the past week. Tito jokingly asked them to tone it down as he arrived at the table with a pot of hot coffee.

"You know, Tito," Grant began, "we each feel like we had major breakthroughs this week. I had been struggling to finish a financial plan I was creating for a big prospect. For whatever reason, I couldn't clearly see how to best present the ideas I had for this family. That is, until this week. During my 4D planning I scheduled a few hour-long blocks, no distractions, no wandering over to pester my marketing assistant, just thinking and researching for this plan. I came up with some ideas I had never thought of before. When I met with the prospect to present the plan, I felt more confident than ever. When the presentation was over, they were so blown away by the work I had done that they immediately decided to become new clients. Usually, in situations like that, closing new business takes weeks with multiple appointments. I don't think I would have gotten to the point I did this week if I hadn't implemented the 4D Framework."

"Impressive," Tito commented. "Sounds like you scheduled an appointment with yourself. That's the compounding effect of the 4D Framework. You ended up with more time, it sounds like you enjoyed putting the plan together, and you served your clients to the best of your ability. Win-win-win."

"The other thing I discovered," Grant continued, "is that I was letting my appointments with my clients and prospects rule my days. As a financial planner, I can have as many as five one-hour meetings per day. And quite often I didn't follow-up on my to-dos because I would leave one appointment, look at my calendar to see who was next, and then start thinking about that meeting. Any open time that I had in between was going to last-minute appointment prep. Now when I schedule time to prep for appointments, I decided to do it in batches, so I'm taking a focused hour to prep for all the day's meetings rather than prepping piecemeal in between. That means I can be better prepared for each meeting and still have time in between appointments to do other important work."

"Here in the diner," Tito commented, "my days are built in large part around the breakfast and lunch rushes. I don't schedule a lot of meetings the way Grant does, but I do have recurring responsibilities like ordering supplies and managing schedules. And like you, Grant, I've found that taking time at the beginning of the day to prepare for my scheduled responsibilities works out better than trying to rush around in between. Each of our daily routines is very different, and the type of tasks that show up on our to-do lists can vary a great deal too. The 4D Framework is designed to be flexible."

"That makes perfect sense," Grant said. "I'm all in on the 4D

Framework. This week I'm going to apply it to my email inbox, and who knows where else it might go from there?"

Nuria spoke up next.

"As you might guess," she said, "based on last week's conversation, I focused first on my email inbox. I can't be certain, but I'd estimate I saved at least an hour of time each day. Instead of interrupting my day by constantly checking my inbox, I blocked off two half-hour email management sessions: once in the morning as the day got started, and then again in the middle of the afternoon. I never needed the full thirty minutes. And as the week went along, I responded to fewer emails and received fewer emails. I even had time to send some of the more proactive emails to clients that I had been putting off. The pace of my days changed; everything I did seemed much less frantic. And the important emails that I did need to answer received better, more thorough replies. It was like magic."

"Wow," Bo jumped in, "I can't wait to try that this week."

"I highly recommend it," Nuria replied, "but I wasn't finished. Since I was already getting time back because of my email routine, I decided to apply the 4D Framework to my to-do list as well. And even though I told you I had good control over my to-do list when we met last week, I found that I was wrong. I thought I had a decent system, but it really wasn't that efficient."

"What were you doing before?" Tito asked.

"I had an app on my phone where I could load all of my tasks and break them down by people, topics, or projects. And then each day as I had time I would go through the whole list and decide what to do next. But I've realized that actually kept me from prioritizing what was most important. I ended up doing whatever felt best in the moment. And I never deleted anything, so my list would get longer and longer every day. I'd have to scroll through an ever-growing list of to-dos every time I was looking for my next task. That was a waste of time. With the 4D Framework, I can stay much more focused."

"Are you still using your app?" Grant asked.

"Yes, I am. I've just set it up in a totally different way. It seems to be working great."

"Good to hear. I've been using a yellow pad for my to-do list for years," Grant remarked, "and I'm going to keep using it. Seems the 4D Framework doesn't require a fancy system as long as you follow the process."

"In the end," Nuria concluded, "I was able to use the time I had gained to get several sales proposals out more quickly than I had planned. I also got a chance to spend more time with a few key members of my team I had been overlooking as I hid in my office. Even though it had been only a few days, each one of them told me they noticed something different about me. They said I seemed happier. That was a real wake-up call. Even though I like to hide behind my computer screens, I pride myself on teamwork, and I discovered another example of how I had been letting them and myself down. Like you said, the 4D Framework has a compounding effect and it kicks in quickly."

As Nuria finished her report, the group heard Bo let out a big breath.

"Are you okay?" Tito asked Bo.

"Yes and no," Bo answered. "First, I have to admit that I was wrong. My preconceived notions that the 4D Framework couldn't work were completely off base. And I don't think it's because all the other things I tried before wouldn't have worked;

it was because I didn't really give them my best effort. Like you suggested, it begins with daily planning."

"Thanks for saying that, Bo," Tito said. "And don't worry; we don't have any crow in the kitchen."

"That's very gracious," Bo said humbly, "but I'd happily eat crow in return for all that I've learned this week. You see, I learned this week that I was sacrificing my family, my business, and my happiness by not taking fifteen minutes a day to plan. Fifteen lousy minutes. I couldn't believe that such a small amount of time could have such a huge impact. Looking back, I now see that my resistance to daily planning was driven by fear. I thought I knew better than everyone else and was afraid to admit that I needed help. I didn't want to admit there were people smarter than me who had already figured out how to manage their time.

"Do you remember the sleepless night we all shared before our first breakfast? I was losing sleep because I had lost control of my time. I was trying to make my days longer and thought I could just grind it out. But the truth is, I just needed a system to understand how I was spending my time. It's embarrassing how simple it all turned out to be."

"Was there something in particular that happened this past week that has you feeling so strongly?" Tito asked.

"Yes, several somethings happened. My first couple of days using the 4D Framework were a disaster. Things actually got worse, but I learned a lot about myself and how others were viewing my time. I'll spare you the details.

"In the past, I would have given up after having a couple of bad days trying something new. Fortunately, I stuck with it and had a huge breakthrough over the next few days. The biggest trick for me was realizing that organizing a list of to-dos that contained so much fluff was impossible. I'd arrange and rearrange things but never took anything off my list. I tried to juggle more balls than humanly possible. But once I committed to deleting the truly unnecessary and delegating to others who were better suited to handle some of my tasks, I had more of an opportunity to get to the stuff that really mattered.

"On top of that, there was a huge bonus. Over each of the past few days, someone close to me has approached me to let me know that they noticed something different about me. The folks I work with most closely noticed almost immediately. The one who surprised me the most was my wife, Maddie. Last night, she asked me if I was okay. She wondered if something was wrong, because I wasn't normally so present with her and the kids when I got home from work. Plus, I'd gotten home early. She told me that most nights I seemed distracted, like my mind was still on what was going on at work. It was hard to admit she was right.

"We ended up having a long conversation about the things that were important to us, and I even had a chance to share my big dream with her. She told me she would support me one hundred percent. We both agreed it was a journey that our family needed to be on together, so we had to be mindful of not taking each other for granted. I think the 4D Framework will help me become an even better husband and father. I know that sounds sappy and we're only two weeks into our journey, but I'm hoping the accountability that comes from our Truest Fan Roundtable and my commitment to being the best husband and father I can be will make achieving my big dream even more rewarding because it will include the people I love the most."

The table fell silent for a moment.

"Thanks for allowing yourself to be so vulnerable," Tito said finally. "It's not always easy to share the things that we discover about ourselves."

"You're right," Bo responded, "but as I was listening to Grant and Nuria talking about what they discovered this past week, it only seemed fair that I do the same even though it seemed to hit me at a deeper emotional level."

"The Truest Fan journey is filled with those kinds of revelations," Tito affirmed. "No, they don't happen every week. Mostly they happen when you least expect them. It's part of the journey of living more purposefully."

"I'm glad you said that," Nuria observed, "because I want to keep this from becoming a phase where I get some quick initial results and then they don't last. You know, like beginning a new exercise routine and feeling good for a few weeks, but then you stop doing it. The initial buzz wears off and you're left with an empty hangover."

"The truth is," Tito continued, "that can happen with the Truest Fan Blueprint just as easily as with any other new system. The blueprint and the roundtable will only be as effective as the effort you consistently give them. And new success routines like the 4D Framework are just as easy to stop doing as they were for you to start doing them. You skip a day or a couple of days for what you think is a good reason, and next thing you know you're totally offtrack. It's happened to me more than once. The good news is, I have my weekly roundtable meetings. It usually doesn't take long for somebody to spot the fact that I've broken a commitment that I've made to them and to myself, and they help put me back on track. My roundtable partners are both coaches and cheerleaders. They're important ingredients in my journey to be the absolute best version of myself."

"I don't want to spoil all the fun of talking about what we've already accomplished," Grant interrupted, "but I think it's important that we talk about what's next. This breakfast can't last forever."

"Right on," Tito replied. "We need to keep the momentum going. I want you to work on two things this week. First, I'd like you to reinforce the 4D Framework both by continuing to implement it the way that you already have and also by adding it to another aspect of your business or life. Bo and Grant, since you didn't try it with your email inboxes, that's probably the most logical next step. Nuria, you're ahead of the game; you could just continue to refine what you're doing with both your to-do list and your email inbox, or, if you're feeling ambitious, you could look for a new way to implement the 4D Framework."

"I actually have an idea about that," Nuria said happily.

"You're just trying to be the teacher's pet," Bo joked.

"Maybe," Nuria shot back. "I can handle the ridicule."

"What's your idea?" Tito asked.

"I want to apply it to my team meetings," she answered. "My team, both the staff in my office and those who support us virtually, meet weekly for what is often a long and unproductive meeting. Our agenda is too busy, and we don't have a good system for focusing on what's most important that week. I'm thinking about introducing the 4D Framework during this week's meeting and suggesting we use that framework to organize our agenda each week as we get started. That way we have a better chance of focusing on the things that are most important. And I'll bet the meetings are a lot shorter."

"Sounds like a great idea," Tito responded. "I would give it a try."

CHAPTER 11

# QUICK WINS

**AFTER THEY EACH AGREED** on how they would continue to implement the 4D Framework, Tito began to introduce the next step in the Truest Fan Blueprint.

"While I go to check on the rest of my customers," he started, "I want you to do a simple exercise. Now that you've recaptured some time in your days, I want you to fill it with a project or an activity that will give your business an almost immediate boost—a Quick Win. Often I find that these Quick Wins relate to sales or marketing. I think it's because many business owners and entrepreneurs get so caught up in the day-to-day of their businesses that they don't keep as focused on growth as they would like. Even when growth is a big part of their future plans."

"I can definitely relate to that," Bo offered, "and I'm in the marketing business. I get so caught up on my clients' projects that I forget to work on my own. I would probably be my own worst client."

"That's pretty common," Tito offered, "but let's see if we can start to fix that this week. Look at your business and your marketing from the inside out. When many businesses look for new sales opportunities, they think about the biggest and boldest and most expensive thing that they could do. They're looking for the Holy

Grail of sales funnels. It's probably because it's easier to think of some big, grand plan for finding new clients than it is to see the opportunities that are right in front of you. Instead of taking action on the obvious, there's a tendency to procrastinate and daydream about all the possibilities that could come from creating the next great marketing and sales campaign. But that new funnel never gets started; it's always something that's put off into the future."

"I see that all the time with my clients," Bo said. "They'll come to me with a really big, outsized idea for increasing sales and once we discuss what's really needed, the solution is usually much simpler."

"Are you talking about me?" Grant asked with a wry smile. "I'm the world's greatest at coming up with outlandish ideas. And you've seen me in my laboratory concocting schemes to impress my client advisory board."

"You're right," Bo replied. "I've seen you at work. You're good, but you're definitely not alone. We'll get you straightened out.

"But let's keep going. I'm curious, Tito, what do you mean about looking at things from the inside out?"

Tito explained, "The outside is that whole big universe of people that you don't know and they don't know you, a cold audience. Finding your target prospects there and converting them into clients can take a lot of time, money, and effort. You rarely get it exactly right the first time you try. It can be a slow process of testing and retesting and testing again. On the other hand, the inside is the people you already know, who could either be clients or could introduce you to potential clients. When you start on the inside looking for referrals, introductions, and strategic partners, you'll find real opportunities."

Grant jumped in. "When we decided to form this roundtable, one of our ideas was to improve our networking. So this seems to be a natural extension of that part of what we set out to do."

"Absolutely," Bo agreed. "This is right up my alley."

"Well, I'll leave you to it," Tito said happily, "but don't be overly ambitious when you start brainstorming. You'll come up with a big list of ideas. There will be a temptation to try to start a bunch of them at the same time. For now, just commit to one strategy that you will each implement this week with the idea of creating a Quick Win for your business."

"Don't worry," Nuria said, "I'll keep them on task. After all, isn't that what the teacher's pet is supposed to do? Let's get down to business. I'd like to go first if you don't mind."

"By all means," Grant said, "it sounds like you already have a project that you'd like to tackle this week."

"I do," Nuria said. "I want to get at least three meetings set up with prospective clients. I have some ideas, but I'm not exactly sure where to start."

"Good stuff," Bo said. "A few additional client meetings would be really helpful for me."

"They say that three's company," Grant joked. "I can easily agree to make holding a few extra meetings a new top priority for the coming week for me too."

"Great," Bo said. "And, well, Tito suggested that we work from the inside to the outside. So I think I need to talk to a few of my clients and ask for referrals. I'm working with a couple of great companies in industries where I'd really like to spend more of my time. I'm going to make getting together with them for coffee my new top priority for the coming week."

"Yeah," Grant chimed in, "I know from experience you're really good at forging connections. If you put your mind to it, I bet you'll have at least a couple of introductions before we get together next week."

"That settles it," Bo concluded. "I have my marching orders. How about you, Nuria?"

"I have several prospects on my list that I've been putting off," Nuria answered. "They're excellent potential clients who have said they want to talk further, but for some reason I haven't gotten back to them yet. Maybe because I was so overwhelmed with emails and tasks off my to-do list. I bet we all have prospects that slip through the cracks from time to time."

"I know I do," Grant agreed. "For now, though, I want to focus on building my centers of influence. You know, other professionals, like accountants and attorneys, who work with the same ideal client as I do and could make professional introductions. My pipeline of active prospects is in pretty good shape, and I'm doing a decent job of getting referrals from clients, but I've let my network of other professionals go stale."

"I think that's another great strategy for working from the inside," Bo agreed. "Do you have a concrete goal for what you want to accomplish?"

"In the past," Grant responded, "I've found that by asking my clients about the other professionals they work with I can source some new centers of influence. But for some reason, I don't always do what works. I get so busy during my client meetings that I forget to put this topic on the agenda. And I'm so busy trying to come up with new marketing ideas that I don't do the simple stuff. It's like self-sabotage. So during each of my client review meetings this week, I'm going to add another item to my agenda for talking to them about other professionals they work with who could be centers of influence. I'll ask them if they would highly recommend their attorneys or accountants or other professional relationships. If they would, then I'll have a list of potential centers of influence with whom I have a mutual client. That makes it easy to schedule future introductory meetings."

"I love that approach," Bo agreed. "When you call on a professional and tell them that your client recommended them, they're flattered. They're almost certain to take a quick meeting to get to know you. More than likely, they could also use introductions from you. That way your center of influence relationships become a two-way street."

"I'm blown away by this conversation," Nuria commented. "Look at how little time it's taken for each of us to come up with a good strategy for developing new business opportunities over the course of the next week. When I leave it to my own devices, I seem to just juggle ideas and find excuses why each one won't work."

"I think that's why Tito put us on the clock," Bo replied. "It's like that silly saying I was once taught during a sales training workshop, that action-takers are money-makers."

The hokey turn of phrase gave them all a good laugh.

Just then, Tito sat back down at the booth and asked them what was so funny.

"Bo was just telling us that action-takers are money-makers," Grant answered.

"Well, I agree," Tito said, "it is a funny saying, but it gets to the very heart of the matter. Ideas, even great ideas, cannot work without action. That's why I encouraged each of you to settle on one important Quick Win for the coming week. How did you do?"

They each relayed their ideas. "I was just telling the others," said Nuria, "I was surprised how quickly we were able to make our plans, probably because we're not so stressed out anymore. Not rushing around all the time, not being distracted—feels great, doesn't it?"

"The teacher's pet gets another A plus," Tito joked. "That's why we worked on the 4D Framework before we started to set new goals and priorities. If we did it the other way around, you would just be compounding any time management challenges you already had."

"Well, we only have a couple of minutes left," Grant said. "What's next?"

Tito pulled out another oversized index card. At the top on the front were the words "Important Work"; the bottom of the card said, "Look for Quick Wins." The Truest Fan motto appeared below, just as on the prior cards.

"I think you know what to do," Tito said. "This week, you should expand your use of the 4D Framework. Plus, write the strategy that you just came up with on the back of this card. Use it as a reminder throughout the week to hold yourself accountable. Let's not pretend that when you leave our breakfast you're going to be totally rid of all the things that could get in the way of getting your most important stuff done. Put your commitments into writing."

"Full speed ahead," Bo cheered. "I can't wait to come back next week and hear about our accomplishments."

## IMPORTANT WORK

## LOOK FOR QUICK WINS

*WE LIVE TO LOVE, TO SERVE, AND TO LEAD OTHERS WITH PURPOSE AND IMPACT.*

CHAPTER 12

# GRANT CAN'T LET GO OF HIS GRAND PLAN

**A FEW DAYS LATER,** Grant sat alone in his office, staring out the window. Despite the confidence he had expressed during breakfast, he didn't feel at ease with his current assignment.

There seemed to be something in his DNA that kept him from sticking with things that worked. He once had a wonderful seminar system that generated new clients every time he used it, but he stopped running the seminars because he got tired of making the same presentation over and over again. He could also recall several other times in his career where he was using a strategy that worked well, but he got bored and stopped doing it.

He'd said he was going to work on a center of influence strategy for his Quick Win campaign, but he frequently got frustrated with the other professionals in his network. He was a natural networker and often made introductions between his clients and his professional peers. He never deliberately gave those introductions because he expected something in return, but in truth he hoped that those to whom he referred business would reciprocate in some way, and very few did. A lot of referrals and introductions went out, but only a trickle came back in. Didn't that mean his Quick Win was doomed before it even started?

Grant had a meeting with his client advisory board on Friday, and he'd already decided to continue pushing the marketing plan they had rejected last time. He knew it was going to be like pounding his head against the wall, but that's just the way he was, and he wasn't sure he really wanted to change—even though he felt like he was being disloyal to his newly formed Truest Fan Roundtable.

As the advisory board meeting got closer, he spent an inordinate amount of time getting ready with his big pitch, falling away from the good habits he had followed last week thanks to the 4D Framework. That made him feel even more guilty, but try as he might, he couldn't think about anything but the pitch.

His overly-thorough prep also took him away from his family. He worked later, and when he was home, he was thinking about the presentation. He wasn't present for his wife and children, even as Bo's words echoed in his head. Bo had been so excited about managing his business better because it let him be more present for his family, and here was Grant doing the opposite. It wasn't the business that was keeping him out of balance, though; it was his desire to prove everybody wrong, that he was capable of pulling off this giant marketing miracle that would revolutionize his business.

He knew he could easily hold a few meetings with centers of influence to fulfill his promise to the roundtable, even while putting most of his energy into his pitch. But he wondered if he would really give it his best. Once again, he found himself losing sleep. His ambition was getting in the way of doing what he knew was most important, and he knew he didn't have a good reason for it.

He wondered how he was going to face his roundtable friends. He guessed Tito would really let him have it. Why did he always have to make things so difficult for himself?

CHAPTER 13

# OUR HEROES ACHIEVE QUICK WINS

**AS THE TRIO** gathered again the following week, Tito heard all of the excitement at their table and rushed over with a pot of hot coffee.

"Keep it down, keep it down," he jokingly scolded. "Some of my other guests haven't even woken up yet. You can see who I'm talking about—they look like they just hit the snooze button."

Everyone laughed.

Bo, as he was apt to do, spoke up quickly. "I had an amazing week, Tito, thanks to you. I can't remember ever being more productive, and I received some of the best introductions that I have ever received."

"No thanks necessary," Tito offered. "You did the work. Tell us more."

"First, if you don't mind a bit of a brag, I think I'm becoming a bit of a 4D Framework ninja. Not only is my to-do list manageable, but I rarely have more than an email or two in my inbox at the end of the day. I find myself looking forward to my planning time and my email management time each day. In some ways, I'm treating it like a game. It's kind of like golf—the lower the score, the better. But instead of birdies and eagles, I'm after as few to-dos and emails as possible."

"We knew you could do it," Grant complimented. Though he looked a little less energetic than the others, he was genuinely proud of his friend's success. "Tell us about the introductions you received."

"Again, not trying to brag," Bo replied, "but it almost seemed too easy. And Tito, you were a witness, whether you realized it or not. Most everybody in town loves coming to Tito's Diner for a cup of your special coffee, so I simply called five clients and offered to meet them here. Of course, folks are busy, so only two were able to meet this past week. I'll be meeting with the others over the next few weeks. So my first win was scheduling five meetings with five key contacts over the course of a few weeks. Sometimes it takes me a month or two to have that many high-quality introductory meetings. The second win was the number of introductions I received during the meetings that I've had so far. In the first meeting, I received just one introduction. But in the second I received three. And I've already scheduled a meeting with one of my new prospective clients. I'll follow up with the rest this week. If I had that kind of success each week, I might not even be able to keep up with the flow of new business."

"Wow," Tito remarked with a grin. "I guess action-takers really are money-makers."

"I've been at this a while," Bo said, "so I know not to count my chickens before they hatch, but I think I'm safe in saying this was a very successful week for future business development."

"Absolutely," Nuria said. "I'm inspired by the energy that you're putting into your efforts. You're setting a great example for all of us."

"Thanks," Bo replied, "but I wouldn't be doing this if we

hadn't all agreed to get one hundred percent behind our Truest Fan Roundtable. How did you do last week, Nuria?"

"I had a great week too," Nuria answered. "My 4D process with my to-do list and my email inbox is continuing to get better, and my team loved the idea of a 4D Framework for our weekly meetings. We're struggling a little bit with the implementation, because bad habits are hard to break, but we think we know how we'll get there. The other really cool thing is that a number of my teammates have also decided to give the 4D Framework a try with their to-dos and emails. I guess, in my own little way, I'm spreading the Truest Fan gospel."

"Very good, grasshopper," Tito quipped. "The more you share the ideas we're learning and putting into action, the more productive your team will be and the more your business will grow. What about your plan to schedule meetings with your stalled prospects?"

"That was a little tougher than I thought," Nuria admitted. "As I suspected, neglecting to follow up with some of them earlier has led to a few closed doors. My prospects had already found somebody else to do the work. That kind of stings. But the good news is that out of seven potential clients I contacted, three of them scheduled time with me. I was able to meet with one of them this past week and the other two are on the books for later this month. If I maintain this level of activity, I'll end up with a pretty big basketful of projects to choose from. Instead of having to take on any project that comes my way, I could be more selective."

"You know what they say about action-takers," Bo snickered, unable to help himself.

"Well, I guess it's my turn," Grant said reluctantly. "I almost blew it. I almost let you all down."

"What do you mean?" Nuria asked with genuine concern. "You do look a little down in the dumps."

"I had a meeting scheduled with my client advisory board this past week. As you may recall, they were the ones giving me real pushback on the massive marketing overhaul I was proposing. I had originally planned to go into the meeting and push for it again. Don't ask me why. I think it was my ego, I felt like I had something to prove. Thankfully, though, after a few fitful nights and a serious session of self-reflection, I decided to put my plans on the back burner.

"Instead, I shared with them the work we've been doing during our breakfasts, especially the idea of my meeting with more centers of influence to uncover new business opportunities. They all looked at me like I was a complete stranger. Not because they didn't like my idea, but because I'd finally realized what they'd been telling me all along—that I'd been trying to reinvent the wheel by chasing all of those bright, shiny objects. Introductions from centers of influence are frustrating for me, but I'm very good at networking, and it's also something all my board members have helped me with over the years. A couple of members of the advisory board were actually introduced to me through other professionals.

"As we were talking, I could feel my face turning red, not because I was angry, but because I was embarrassed that I had ignored all my board members' great advice for so long. I asked them to advise me because I knew that they could help me and they had my best interests at heart, but then I didn't want to hear what they had to say—until now, when it finally clicked. The worst part," Grant continued, "was once again letting my ego get in my way. Sometimes I can be my own worst enemy."

"What do you mean by that?" Nuria asked.

"I'm always overreaching," Grant replied. "No matter how often I tell myself to put first things first, I'm always trying to skip a step. It's a self-inflicted wound that zaps my energy and leads to periods of overwhelm and frustration.

"To make matter worse, setting priorities is one of the most important lessons I teach my clients as I guide them through their financial plans. We always talk about the importance of putting goals in proper perspective and order. Focus on the things that truly matter the most.

"Most importantly, my impetuousness doesn't impact just me; it impacts those who work and live around me. At work it drags down my team. I'm frequently throwing them off course by redirecting them from the projects they're working on—often at the last minute with little regard for deadlines.

"At home I'm regularly so caught up thinking about work that I'm not paying attention to the people who are most important in my life. My zest for finding the next great idea completely thwarts my work-life balance. I may be at home at a reasonable time most evenings, but the quality of that time can be awful. I might be present at my kids' events at school, but I'm not truly engaged."

"Hold on, hold on," Bo interrupted. "I understand where you're coming from. After all, I'm the workaholic in this group. You need to give yourself a break. The work we're doing in our roundtable will help you get on track."

"Bo is absolutely right," Tito added. "When you put in the work, you'll learn more and more about yourself. Most of it will be good, but sometimes you also uncover the chinks in your armor. The ways your bad habits and sloppy thinking are impacting the people around you."

"I've already seen it firsthand," Nuria interjected. "My self-isolation wasn't just a problem for me; I told you how it cost me a big client. But you can't fix a problem until you know you have one, and thankfully I'm already experiencing breakthroughs as I change my ways."

"Thanks," Grant replied. "I appreciate all of your cheerleading. You're reminding me to look at the glass as half-full and not as half-empty. Maybe the flip side of overreaching is being overly critical."

"Good point," Tito said. "Now tell us how your week ended up."

"Fortunately, after I made the decision to change my approach with the board, I was able to get back on track. Even with the self-inflicted interruption, I definitely got a lot more done in a lot less time. I also had success in asking my clients for introductions to their other professional advisors. I held five client reviews, and included professional introductions as part of the agenda. Every one of my clients was happy to help me and when I add it all up, I ended up with eight potential centers of influence for follow-up. I've already scheduled a couple of breakfast meetings, so make sure you reserve my booth for me all next week, Tito."

"I'll put a plaque on it," Tito offered, "and you may even gain membership into our exclusive frequent flyer club if you're not careful. So what are you missing?"

"I dropped the ball on applying the 4D Framework to my email routine," Grant confessed. "I only had a couple of days to try it, and each day I ended up being unable to avoid the temptation of answering emails as the notifications came up on my computer and cell phone. Those rings, dings, and wooshes are hard to ignore."

"Let me give you some help, Grant," Bo offered. "Turn the notifications off. If you're using the 4D Framework for managing your email, you don't need them."

"Wow, look at Mr. Organization," Nuria teased. "Maybe you'll become the new teacher's pet. If I'm not careful, I'll be out of a job."

"All kidding aside," Tito cut in, "sometimes we miss the obvious when we're trying new routines. And that's another reason the accountability of these roundtables is so important. One day you're the student and the next day you're the teacher."

"What's next?" Nuria asked excitedly.

"Before we move to the next step," Tito answered, "let's do a quick recap of what you've accomplished. First, you each have a big dream, a picture of what your future success will look like. You're beginning to treat it as a magnet that will help pull you into the future—a destination toward which you're headed, even if you don't know the exact path you'll take."

"That's a great reminder," Grant interrupted. "Even though it's only been a few weeks, I can see that I've gotten so excited about my short-term progress that I haven't reminded myself of my big dream in a while."

"Good point," Tito replied. "It's easy to lose focus even when things are going well. That's one of the reasons I had you place your big dream on one of the cards. The cards you're completing aren't just for doing the exercises. I hope you'll refer to them regularly. I like to review my big dream every day, imagining I am now a day closer to making it come true.

"The second thing we've covered," Tito continued, "is the 4D Framework. You're using it as a tool both to help you create more time for your most important priorities and as a way for sorting what matters most. You've used the framework with your to-do list and your email inbox. And Nuria, you even found a way to use it in team meetings. Definitely one of the most important tools in the Truest Fan toolbox."

"I'm keeping it right next to my hammer and screwdriver," Bo joked. "I don't know how I ever lived without it."

"And third," Tito cut in, not wanting to interrupt the flow of his review, "you learned the importance of looking for Quick Wins. You've taken the time that you've uncovered through better time management and you're spending it on an activity that will help you accomplish an important priority. So far, those have mostly related to sales and business development activities. As time moves along, you'll find other ways to apply the same habit."

"To tell you the truth," Grant interjected, "even if we stop here and just repeatedly use what we've learned so far during our roundtable sessions, I think we'd make great progress."

"You're right," Tito said. "You've established a great foundation. Now it's time to start building on top of that foundation so you can get even more out of your partnership."

"What's our next assignment?" Nuria asked. "I'm sure we're all ready to continue on this journey."

CHAPTER 14

# GAME PLAN

**"I'M GLAD YOU ASKED,"** Tito answered, placing a sheet of blank paper in front of each of them. "Let's connect the dots between what you've been accomplishing in the short run and the big dream that you have pictured for the future. On this paper, I want you to allow your imaginations to run wild. Think about all the milestones you'll accomplish over the next three years and write them down. They could be business milestones that relate to hitting financial targets, building a team, new services you'll offer to your clients, or anything else that may be on your mind. They could also be personal milestones. Hopes you have for yourself or for your family or for the involvement that you want to have with the causes that you care about. Don't try to put them in order; just create a list. The length doesn't matter. When I come back to the table, I'll give you some instructions on what to do with it."

"This seems a lot like the Dream Big exercise," Grant pointed out.

"I can understand why you might say that," Tito responded. "It is similar. I don't want you to hold anything back from your brainstorming. The difference is that milestones are the roadmap toward your big dreams. They're goals and objectives that you feel you need to accomplish to take the next steps in your business as you journey through the next few years."

"We've trusted you so far," Bo remarked, "and you haven't let us down. I'm ready to give this a try."

"Teacher's pet," Nuria offered with a big grin. "I'm happy to pass the reins."

The trio grabbed their pens and got to work.

About ten minutes later, when Tito returned, Nuria, Grant, and Bo were all still furiously writing.

"Well," Tito began, "it doesn't seem like you're having any trouble with this exercise. Time to put your pens down." He paused, chuckling. "Sorry, that's my inner test proctor coming out again. I just can't seem to help myself."

"I'm glad you stopped me," Nuria said. "My hand was beginning to cramp. I'm happy to take a break."

"Me too," Grant agreed.

Bo asked for more time.

"That's all for now, Bo," Tito said. "This is your list, so you can come back to it and add to it anytime you want."

"Good to know," Bo said. "Now I'm wondering what we're going to do with it."

"Let me guess," Grant suggested eagerly, "we're going back to delete, delegate, defer, and do. Am I right?"

"Looks like Grant wants to have his chance at being the teacher's pet," Bo offered with a laugh.

"Takes one to know one," Grant shot back.

"Well," Tito replied, "that's part of it, but there's more."

He then handed each of them three cards. The first one read

"One Year" at the top, the second read "Three Years," and the third read "Unknown."

"This week," Tito continued, "you're going to begin building your Game Plan, step four of the Truest Fan Blueprint. I want you to read back over the list you've been working on and place each item on one of these cards. On the first card, you're listing the milestones you want to accomplish within the next year. On the second, the milestones you have for the next three years. And finally, anything you're not sure of, place on the third card."

"Where does the 4D Framework come into play?" Nuria asked.

"Great question," Tito answered. "Here's how I'd like you to approach this exercise. As you're going through your list, feel free to delete anything that isn't important. I'm sure you've each written down some milestones that may duplicate others or, as you review them, don't make sense now that you're concentrating on creating one-year and three-year milestones. So delete those. For now you're going to take on all your milestones personally. So don't worry so much about delegating, although I'm sure as you begin to put your milestones into action, you'll have opportunities to delegate some aspects of them to members of your teams. Think of your one-year card as your 'do' list and your three-year card as your 'defer' list. The unknown card is for things that you believe will be important milestones for your business, but you're not ready to put them into a one-year or a three-year timeline. Over time, as you repeat this exercise, you'll be able to go to your unknown list and decide when it's time to add an item to one of your milestone lists, or maybe even delete it."

"Dividing this list up will be harder than making it in the first place," Grant offered.

"It will certainly take more time than we have this morning," Tito replied, "and that's another reason why we've already worked on freeing up time for your most important activities. I want you to make this exercise a big priority for the coming week. Block off at least a couple of sessions to take a crack at it. You can do a draft of your cards in your first session and then come back to it a day or two later to clean it up. And when we get together next week, I'll show you how to use these milestone cards going forward."

"Should we separate our personal and professional milestones?" Bo asked.

"Not for now," Tito answered. "We'll talk about that more next week."

"I'm concerned that I won't be able to separate my one-year and three-year milestones," Grant offered. "As you all know, one of my biggest challenges is trying not to bite off more than I can chew. That's particularly true when I'm thinking about short-term priorities. I can imagine my one-year list overflowing while there is very little on my three-year list."

"I'm glad you're self-aware about what you might struggle with," Tito responded. "Just do your best, and next week we'll help you sort that out."

## ONE YEAR

**YOUR GAME PLAN IS THE ROADMAP LEADING TO YOUR BIG DREAMS.**

*"WE LIVE TO LOVE, TO SERVE, AND TO LEAD OTHERS WITH PURPOSE AND IMPACT."*

## THREE YEARS

## YOUR GAME PLAN IS THE ROADMAP LEADING TO YOUR BIG DREAMS.

*"WE LIVE TO LOVE, TO SERVE, AND TO LEAD OTHERS WITH PURPOSE AND IMPACT."*

## UNKNOWN

**YOUR GAME PLAN IS THE ROADMAP LEADING TO YOUR BIG DREAMS.**

*"WE LIVE TO LOVE, TO SERVE, AND TO LEAD OTHERS WITH PURPOSE AND IMPACT."*

CHAPTER 15

# NURIA'S FEELINGS OF ISOLATION RETURN

**NURIA SAT AT HER DESK,** staring at her planner. She had scheduled some time with herself to work on her goals, but as she got started, she quickly realized that the overconfidence she had felt during the breakfast meeting was unfounded. The list she needed to prioritize felt much longer and more imposing than when she first created it. She felt alone, as she almost always did when facing a challenge.

She was used to isolating herself and orchestrating events from the background, like a puppeteer. But now she wanted to become a better leader, someone who could develop a set of goals that would lead to her big dream. She wanted her team and her clients to aspire to that dream as well. She also needed to tie her goals to the ways she wanted to improve things at home.

The Dream Big exercise had inspired her to be the best version of herself, to become a leader so that her business could be the best that it could be. She hoped that, when the time came for her to walk away from the business, it would be able to run without her. She wanted to pass it along to those teammates who had been so loyal to her.

But she also knew how easy it would be to drift away from those dreams and into her old bad habits. Isolating herself, not including her team, and not keeping her family in mind. She couldn't let that happen. Her commitment to helping kids in some yet-unknown way needed to be part of her decision-making, even if she didn't act on it in the next year.

The time she had set aside to work on the cards was over before she knew it, and she felt like she hadn't put a dent in what she set out to do. This was going to be much harder than she thought. But she'd scheduled more time with herself for tomorrow; she could come back to her cards then with fresh eyes. She didn't want to let down Tito and the rest of the Truest Fan Roundtable.

As she closed her planner, she couldn't shake the feeling that she was alone in this. She wished she could talk to someone who understood what she was going through, who could offer her guidance and support. But she didn't want to burden her team or her family with her worries.

She had to find a way to overcome her fears and doubts and become the leader she wanted to be. It wasn't going to be easy, but she was determined to do it.

CHAPTER 16

# OUR HEROES' GAME PLANS COME TO LIFE

**UNUSUALLY,** Tito was waiting for them at their favorite booth when the trio arrived for the following week's breakfast.

Once they all sat down, Tito jumped right in.

"We have a lot to cover today," Tito began, "so I've been waiting for you. And since you each seem to be creatures of habit, I've already placed your breakfast orders. They should be here any minute."

"Sounds kind of mysterious," Bo offered. "Are we going to learn the secret Truest Fan handshake today?"

"No, that doesn't come until week twelve," Tito replied.

"I was just joking about a secret handshake," Bo remarked in surprise.

"I am too," Tito shot back.

They all had a good laugh.

"Now let's talk about what to do with those milestones you've been creating. Let's start with the one-year card first. Nuria, if you don't mind, tell us what you recorded."

"I don't mind at all," she answered, despite feeling anxious. She was eager to see how the others felt she had done. "I listed five items:

1. Eliminate working nights and weekends by continuously using the 4D Framework for all tasks and projects. This will allow me to be more focused each day at work as well as allow for quality time with my family.
2. Increase sales by twenty-five percent by adding four new major projects, one per quarter. This will require increasing our pipeline of future clients to a minimum of eight.
3. Increase annually recurring revenues by fifty percent by converting ten of our current project-based clients into retainer-based relationships. I will hold meetings with our top twenty-five clients to initiate this process.
4. Develop greater teamwork and a clear vison for our company by clearly articulating our mission and core values. This will lead to creating a system that truly rewards each team member for their contribution and performance.
5. Take an uninterrupted two-week vacation with my family so I have time to rest, recharge, and spend quality time with the people I love most in this world.

"I've done some goal setting in the past," Nuria admitted, "so I think that helped. And after a rough start, I decided to be as clear and efficient as possible. I want goals that are easily understandable as well as attainable for this coming year. I also find that combining professional and personal milestones helps me keep each of them in mind as I look back on them and share them with my family and team."

"Terrific job, Nuria," Tito complimented. "I appreciate the fact that your milestones are concise and attainable within the next twelve months. And they each contain clarifying points that will help you put them into action, while also highlighting your reasons for choosing them."

"That makes me feel much better," Bo chimed in. "The goals I've set for myself over the next year follow a similar pattern, but I don't think I challenged myself enough. If I'm disciplined, I'm sure I can hit more milestones than I've recorded on my one-year card so far."

"I feel much better too," Grant added. "The big reason my one-year card is so long is that I listed lots of small bullet points that could very easily be collapsed into milestone statements like the ones Nuria shared. I'm probably still trying to bite off more than I can chew in twelve months, but I'm much closer than I thought."

"You definitely understand where we're going," Tito said to all three of them. "You're beginning to see that milestones are not the same as a to-do list. They're major accomplishments that you'd like to achieve over the course of the year. They should include clarifying language about how you will do them or why they're so important to you. Nuria's milestones are wonderful examples."

"This is exciting," Bo exclaimed. "I'm beginning to see what's possible for me and my team to achieve in the coming year. I'm also seeing how it relates to being intentional about my time away from work. If I keep my goals in mind, there's a much better chance that my family and my passion projects will get the best from me and not just the leftovers."

"I still think there's something missing," Grant said. "I've set goals before, but I don't usually get them done. I'll talk about them at the beginning of the year and feel great about them. Then I'll look at them again a few months later, like at the end of the first quarter, and I'll have hardly made a dent in them. I usually tell myself something like, 'Well, at least I have nine more months to reach them.' And I just keep procrastinating all year. I end up either scrambling to hit my goals in the last few months of the year or abandoning my goals and trying to convince myself they really weren't important anyway."

"Don't be discouraged," Nuria said. "As much as I like to make it sound like I'm really efficient at hitting my goals and milestones, I usually don't either. The way I react to them and push them off may not be exactly the same as you, but I struggle too."

"Me too," Bo agreed, "but I guess that's no surprise."

"Hold on, hold on," Tito quickly cut in. "This isn't a pity party where we cry over past spilled milk. Setting a Game Plan should help put an end to the frustrations you've been describing."

"Okay, that sounds hopeful," Bo said. "So how *do* we stay on track?"

"Glad you asked," Tito answered. "We're going to work on that right now. Here's a fresh set of Game Plan cards. I'm going to go check on the rest of my customers, and while I'm gone I'd like you to use them to update your Game Plans based on the conversation that we just had. You may not be able to get through all of them, so I want you to start with your one-year card, and then if you have time, start working on the others."

"Tito, before you go," Nuria said, "I'd like to share something else that happened this past week that's directly related to the work we've been doing in our roundtable."

"Sure thing," Tito replied. "Sharing results, good or bad, is an important part of the roundtable process."

"Do you all remember the meeting I scheduled with one of my stalled prospects?" Nuria asked.

"I do," Bo said. "That was one of your Quick Wins last week."

"Yes, it was," she said, "and this week it became an even quicker win. When I met with my prospect and asked how I could help, she told me that she had recently fired her web developer and needed someone else to step in quickly. So the timing of our meeting was absolutely perfect. After discussing her requirements, I was able to recommend someone from my team. Within forty-eight hours, we inked a deal, and this could be one of the top five clients in my agency."

"Sounds almost too good to be true," Bo offered. "I wish I could say that I landed a great new client too, but I haven't. I do have three great new prospects in my pipeline and one top-notch proposal on the drawing board, though. Like Nuria, it's business that wouldn't be in motion if I hadn't taken the time to prioritize it."

"Way to go, you two," Grant cheered. "I'm really proud of you. As much as our meetings may have helped, you both took action and did the work. Remember what they say about action-takers—now you're money-makers."

"I really do need to check on the rest of my customers," Tito said. "I don't mean to minimize your accomplishments. I'm proud of you too."

"We get it, Tito," Grant offered. "Go pour some more coffee for your other guests and we'll get back to work on our Game Plans."

Nuria, Bo, and Grant dove right into their next assignment. None of them spoke for at least ten minutes. Grant was the first to come up for air.

"Wow," he said, "when I went back to my cards things quickly became very clear. I feel great about what I'd like to accomplish over the next twelve months. My three-year milestones are still a little foggy, but I'm sure they'll get clearer as time goes along. My unknown card only has a few items, kind of pie-in-the-sky ideas. Going forward, maybe I'll follow through on them or maybe I won't. At least now I know I'm working toward my big dreams."

"I'm feeling the exact same way," said Nuria. "Maybe it's just because of all the energy we've generated as we've been working together, but now I see an even clearer path forward."

Bo, hesitating slightly, added his thoughts. "My one-year milestones may still be way more than I can handle. I feel like I have a grocery list for a store that doesn't carry everything I need. There's no way I can check everything off the list, because some of the items I want aren't attainable. I can't seem to cut it back and frame my milestones the way that you described yours, Nuria."

"While we're waiting for Tito, let's see if we can help you out," Grant offered. "Give us an idea of where you're struggling."

"Well," Bo replied, "for example, I'd like to increase my company's revenues by one hundred twenty-five thousand dollars. That seems straightforward, but it's just a number. I've thrown around numbers like that for years. I also know that I need to increase the average size of my client relationships because I know that as we grow we'll need to reduce the number of projects we take on while increasing the size of the projects on which we bid and accept. Those ideas seem to tie together, but I can't think of a way to phrase them in my Game Plan."

"Well," Nuria offered, "what's your ideal size for a new client?"

"Right now, "Bo answered. "Our sweet spot is somewhere between ten and fifteen thousand dollars per project. At that price point, we know we have a client who could take advantage of the most important services we offer. Less than that, we have to compromise on what we're able to deliver. And there's no problem if we run into bigger projects; we can handle them comfortably. We've even talked about setting a ten thousand dollar minimum for new relationships, but it's been hard to turn the smaller projects away."

"Let me take a crack at this," Grant offered. "What if you created a milestone that read, 'We will increase our sales by one hundred twenty-five thousand dollars by adding ten new clients who each have a minimum project fee of twelve thousand five hundred dollars. To do this we will always have twenty active prospects in our pipeline who are capable of paying us that minimum fee.'"

"I like it," Nuria agreed. "When you set your goal like that, you're tying the results that you need to get from your sales and marketing efforts to your pipeline, your target for new ideal relationships, and your revenue goal. That's a great equation. When I set goals like that, I tend to exceed my target because my clients end up bringing us average revenues that exceed my minimum. Plus, if I get additional business from our existing clients, that also adds to our total. When we stay focused on a primary income goal that's tied to new business from new relationships, that number becomes our leading indicator."

"Same thing for me," Grant echoed. "I like to get extra revenue from existing relationships, but I try not to count on it. Organic growth is great, but new business from new and bigger clients helps us move forward faster."

"You know," Bo agreed, "that's a great way to frame a revenue goal. And when I think about it, it matches up with the way that I've always viewed my business. I just haven't articulated it the same way. I like to throw a bunch of numbers in the air, and figure if I can knock a few of them off I'll be okay. In truth, a goal like you two suggested is more likely to help me stay focused and not only hit my income goal but also increase the quality of the clients that I serve."

"Do you want to talk through the rest of your one-year milestones?" Grant asked.

"I think I have an idea how to tackle them now," Bo said. "I'm going to take some time to clean them up this week."

"Great," Nuria offered, "and we'll be your sounding board when you're ready. In fact, I bet we'll get a chance to talk about them next week."

Having overheard this last exchange, Tito sat back down, nodding in agreement.

"That's a key responsibility of roundtable partners," he remarked. "You'll be regular sounding boards and problem-solvers for each other."

"I guess that that will be a big part of our ongoing roundtable sessions," Grant added. "Once you help us finish our Truest Fan Roundtable training during these breakfasts, we'll move on to a more regular rhythm of coaching, encouraging, and holding each other accountable."

"You're right," Tito replied. "There's always more you can learn about the process, but putting it into action should become a top priority."

## ONE YEAR

## YOUR GAME PLAN IS THE ROADMAP LEADING TO YOUR BIG DREAMS.

*"WE LIVE TO LOVE, TO SERVE, AND TO LEAD OTHERS WITH PURPOSE AND IMPACT."*

## THREE YEARS

**YOUR GAME PLAN IS THE ROADMAP LEADING TO YOUR BIG DREAMS.**

*"WE LIVE TO LOVE, TO SERVE, AND TO LEAD OTHERS WITH PURPOSE AND IMPACT."*

## UNKNOWN

**YOUR GAME PLAN IS THE ROADMAP LEADING TO YOUR BIG DREAMS.**

*"WE LIVE TO LOVE, TO SERVE, AND TO LEAD OTHERS WITH PURPOSE AND IMPACT."*

CHAPTER 17

# TFAP
## TRUEST FAN ACTION PLAN

**"HOW DO WE TACKLE** these one-year milestones?" Nuria asked. "We can't do them all at once, not even with the extra time we've created through the 4D Framework."

"Very good observation," Tito responded. "That's why I now want to talk with you about creating your first TFAP."

"What's a TFAP?" Bo asked.

"Truest Fan Action Plan," Tito answered.

At this moment, Tito gave each of them a new card. The Truest Fan motto was displayed at the bottom. Just above the motto was the phrase "Your ninety-day action plan." The top of the card featured the abbreviation "TFAP."

"TFAP is Truest Fan lingo for a ninety-day action plan," he explained. "Now that you have greater clarity on your one-year milestones, I want to help you break them down into more actionable pieces. I've found that ninety days is the right amount of time. During your TFAP, you can work on a specific milestone or two, or you can draw action items from several of your milestones. The main idea is that when you get laser-focused on the action items that will make the biggest difference right now, you're likely to get more done. The activities that you choose for the TFAP help you make decisions on a day-to-day basis. You can ask yourself if the things that you're prioritizing during your 4D planning or when you're considering new projects and ideas will help you accomplish the action items you have on your plate for the current TFAP. Your TFAP is both a tool that highlights the things that you will be doing and a barometer for deciding how to handle any unexpected challenges that come up."

"So your TFAP is your 'do' list," Grant offered. "You're looking at your one-year milestones and deciding what you want to work on right now, like the 'do' step of the 4D Framework."

"Exactly," Tito replied, "and you're deferring the other items in your one-year milestone list to future TFAPs. Every ninety days you'll have an opportunity to decide what to do next."

"I love it," Nuria said. "This is just what I was looking for when I said I was concerned about how to tackle my one-year milestones. I've never broken them down this way before."

"That's right," Tito encouraged, "and your TFAPs will be an essential part of your weekly roundtable meetings. They're going to be your best tool for keeping up with the commitments that you make to yourselves, to your businesses, and to each other. We'll get into some of the details on how that will work when we get together next time."

"Uh-oh," Bo joked, "this is going to be some serious accountability."

"Yes sir," Grant fired back. "We're going to hold your feet to the fire!"

"Can't wait," Bo said smugly. "I think the accountability of holding each other to our TFAPs will be the real turning point that'll show whether this roundtable was just another wild self-improvement idea or if we really have a purpose for getting together and drinking Tito's coffee and eating his famous bacon every week."

"You're off to a great start," Tito said. "Your hearts and your minds are definitely in the right place. Your ultimate success will come from sticking with it while knowing that life is certainly going to try to get in the way."

"Thanks for the reality check, Tito," Grant offered. "We all need to try to stay grounded and focused."

"I feel confident that we'll look out for each other," Nuria added. "Over the past few weeks, we've set a great foundation for what we need to do going forward. Don't you think so, Tito?"

"I do," Tito answered. "As we wrap up today, I'm simply going to ask that you each complete your first TFAP and bring it back to next week's breakfast."

# TFAP

## YOUR NINETY-DAY ACTION PLAN.

*"WE LIVE TO LOVE, TO SERVE, AND TO LEAD OTHERS WITH PURPOSE AND IMPACT."*

CHAPTER 18

# BO NEEDS TO CONVINCE HIS TEAM

**AFTER BREAKFAST,** Bo sat in his car, his gaze fixed on the windshield. The thought of adhering to the Truest Fan Action Plan (TFAP) for ninety days left him feeling overwhelmed. Despite this, Bo knew it was crucial, and he committed to making positive changes by calling a team meeting.

As the meeting got started, Bo felt a mix of excitement and apprehension. He was determined to commit to the TFAP and embrace his role as a leader, even if the idea seemed daunting. Bo had always been spontaneous, leading to long nights and frustrations for both him and his team when he made last-minute changes. It was time to establish a clear direction and share his vision with his team.

Bo began the meeting by outlining his goals and vision for the next ninety days, introducing the TFAP he had been working on. This marked a departure from his usual laid-back demeanor, and some team members initially expressed confusion. One key team member even questioned if Bo was joking. Others struggled to believe the words coming from Bo's mouth, wondering if it was just a phase or if the company was in trouble, prompting what felt like drastic steps. They were accustomed to the excitement of chasing Bo's whims and adapting to his ever-changing leadership style.

Bo acknowledged their concerns but remained firm in his decision to adopt the structured TFAP. He knew it was the right thing to do, and if some team members couldn't adjust to the new leadership style, he might need to consider different hiring decisions in the future. This thought made him feel tougher than he had ever been with his team, causing him to wonder again if they would take him seriously.

Throughout the meeting, Bo continued to clearly present the goals and expectations of the TFAP, addressing any confusion or questions. Gradually, the team began to buy in and accept the new direction. By the time the meeting ended, they left with a clear set of objectives, prepared to embark on this new journey together.

Bo felt a sense of relief. He understood that becoming a true leader wouldn't be easy, but he also recognized his team's potential. United, they could face any challenge and achieve great success. The meeting had been a positive step forward, and Bo was eager to see where this new leadership style and the TFAP would take them.

CHAPTER 19

# OUR HEROES COMMIT TO TAKING ACTION

**AS THEY GATHERED** the following week, the trio seemed unusually quiet. "What's wrong?" Tito asked as he approached the table.

"What do you mean?" Nuria questioned in return.

"The last few weeks you've been buzzing with excitement as you've gathered," Tito replied. "What changed? Did the dog eat your proverbial homework?"

"I'm not sure I can pinpoint it exactly," Bo offered, "but for me creating my first TFAP made me feel like I was making a major commitment. We've shared a lot with each other over the past few weeks, but there's something about getting down to work and focusing on our ninety-day action plans that makes it seem more real. Plus, I even shared my TFAP with my team and that was one of the toughest things I've ever done as the leader of my company. I felt like I was having an out of body experience.."

"You probably were, Bo," Nuria teased. "But we love you regardless. Sharing the TFAP with your team is an excellent move. You can't do it alone, and that's coming from someone who's tried."

"I think you're onto something else, Bo," Grant added. "By sharing our TFAPs and asking each other for help with accountability, we're moving from discovering the foundations of the Truest Fan Blueprints to continuous implementation. Our Truest Fan Roundtable is taking a big step forward. I hope we all know what we've gotten ourselves into."

"Well," Tito said, "I'm glad you recognize how important this step is in the development of your roundtable, but don't let it intimidate you. You've been doing a great job so far of grasping the ideas, sharing your thoughts, and taking action on the initial steps. And you seem to be having a lot of fun as you do it. I think you'll find in the coming weeks that it will be just as enjoyable, even if the routines change. If you give your TFAP the same type of energy and enthusiasm as you gave to the first handful of Truest Fan Blueprint steps, you'll do just fine. Besides, I'll be around to keep an eye on you."

"Then let's get to it," Nuria offered. "I don't like this gloomy vibe. Plus, I think I have a great TFAP, if I say so myself."

"That means you're first at bat," Bo said. "After all, you're the original teacher's pet in this group."

Everyone chuckled, and the mood began to lighten.

"Okay, here goes," Nuria continued. "I have six items on my TFAP:

1. I will use the 4D Framework for my to-do list and my email inbox daily.
2. I will leave my office no later than 5:30 at least three days per week.
3. I will schedule at least one meeting with a prospective client each week.
4. I will develop a roadmap that outlines my company's unique client proposition.

5. I will implement a daily stand-up meeting with my team.
6. I will hold weekly pizza parties with my family where we'll talk about the location of our two-week vacation in June."

"That sounds bold and ambitious," Bo commented. "How does your TFAP relate to your one-year milestones?"

"Glad you asked," Nuria replied. "I tried to align them as much as possible. First, since implementing the 4D Framework needs to become an ongoing habit, I decided that I needed to put that commitment in writing.

"Secondly, if I'm serious about not working nights and weekends, I felt I needed to turn that into an action step as well. But I know it will be hard to go cold turkey on staying late, so I decided to start with three days a week.

"As you know from my Quick Wins, more consistently scheduling meetings with prospective clients is very important for growing my business. I believe a good start to making that a regular routine is to commit to having at least one meeting with a future client each week, whether it's an initial information gathering session or a follow-up session. If I have at least one of those meetings each week, my pipeline will almost certainly be where I need it to be by the end of the next ninety days.

"My fourth action step is a project I've been putting off for quite a while. Most of my prospects and clients see my work as standalone projects, but my best outcomes come from working with clients on an ongoing basis. The client journey roadmap I want to create is a system for continuously helping these ongoing clients elevate the results they get in their businesses through the work we do together. It's our unique client proposition. Unfortunately, right now the roadmap only exists in my head. I've never taken the time to document it for use in meetings and presentations."

"May I interrupt you?" Grant asked.

"Sure," Nuria replied.

"We have a roadmap for our business just like what you're talking about. We call it our signature solution; it's how we help our clients get from where they are when we first begin working with them to where they would ultimately like to be as they implement the plan we help them put in place. When we walk a prospective client through our signature solution, I can usually see a lightbulb going on. They stop thinking about us as just someone who helps them with their investments and more like who we truly want to be for them: financial planners and partners on their life's journey."

"To tell you the truth, Grant," Nuria said, "I kind of borrowed my roadmap idea from you. You've shown yours to me before, and I've been mentally adapting it to my business ever since I saw it. It's brilliant. And during this TFAP, I'm finally going to get it done."

"That sounds like a great idea," Bo cheered.

"My fifth priority relates to building a stronger team. When our team is operating at its best, we hold regular daily stand-up meetings. It's the best way to keep tuned in to what each other is doing and reduces the number of times we interrupt each other throughout the day. It's also a great time to ask for and offer help when someone is stuck. We need to make it a habit."

"Great idea," Bo offered. "When we get some time I'd like to talk with you about how you run those stand-up meetings. I bet my team would benefit from something similar."

"Absolutely," Nuria replied. "That's what we're here for! As for my last action item . . . my family and I have already set the date for our big two-week vacation, but we aren't sure where we'd like to go. We've never taken this much time off together. So we've decided to hold a weekly pizza dinner where we'll all bring up ideas for our trip. I think it will be a lot of fun and then when we make our final decision, our collaboration should add to the excitement of our big vacation."

"Bravo!" Tito exclaimed. "You've done a wonderful job of creating a TFAP that addresses your milestones and turns them into actions. And you've also broken it down into bite-sized pieces. Barring unforeseen circumstances, I can see you accomplishing each of those action items over the next ninety days."

"I agree with you, Tito," Grant added. "As I listened to Nuria listing her priorities and then explaining why each one of them was important, I could picture her getting them done. I could also picture her business growing, her team working better together, and her having more time and more fun with her family."

"Ditto," Bo added. "I really like the simplicity and the balance of the activities Nuria has chosen. I'm no expert, but they feel just right for what she's trying to accomplish."

As the breakfast continued, the group reviewed the TFAPs that Grant and Bo had created. Like Nuria, they had done a good job. The only controversy that they ran into was Bo having a list of priorities that seemed unrealistic for ninety days. In the end, they left them alone, deciding that the opportunity to meet and talk about them each week would allow for adjustments along the way.

CHAPTER 20

# ROADBLOCKS

**GAUGING THAT THE GROUP** was where they needed to be with their TFAPs, Tito handed them a new card. The top of the card contained one word: "Roadblocks."

"Roadblocks?" Grant wondered out loud. "I thought our TFAPs were designed to keep us from running into roadblocks."

"They will," Tito said, "but there is no way to avoid them completely. Sometimes challenges come at you from the outside, while other times they come from the inside. Maybe your roadblocks look like changes in the competitive landscape, or maybe you're worried about not staying committed to the things that you have set out to do."

"I know what you mean," Grant replied. "In the investment world, bear markets are always lurking around the corner. When they show up, you have to make adjustments, or you'll get run over.

"And we all have some mental baggage," Grant continued, "those self-defeating thoughts that get in the way of our accomplishments. I'm sure I'm not the only one who has successfully implemented a strategy to improve my business and then for no good reason just decided to stop doing it. It's self-sabotage."

"Great examples," Tito agreed. "It's important to name them. That way you know what to be on the lookout for. And when you share them with the roundtable, your partners will be on the lookout for them too. So while I'm gone, try recording potential roadblocks on your cards."

"Wait," Bo said after a few minutes, "instead of writing down our potential roadblocks before we talk about them, let's just discuss them. I bet we're running into a lot of the same obstacles."

"Okay with me," Nuria said.

"Not me," Grant insisted.

"Wow, that's a surprise," Bo said. "Seems like we already have a roadblock."

They all laughed.

"Listen," Grant began, "I know we're all eager to start discussing, but I think it's important that we really understand what roadblocks are and how they affect us before we dive into specific examples."

Bo and Nuria both nodded in agreement, and Grant continued, "You see, I've been told my whole life to just muscle through things, that roadblocks aren't real, and that I just need to put on my big boy pants. But I don't think that's necessarily true. I think sometimes there are things beyond our control that we need to acknowledge and name. We need to be prepared for their arrival and know how to deal with them—and sometimes accept that they'll slow us down a little."

Bo chimed in, "I can totally relate to that tough-man attitude. I've been guilty of plowing through roadblocks instead of taking the time to really understand and address them."

Nuria nodded in agreement and added, "And as someone

who's used to solving her own problems, I'm not always sure what's a roadblock versus just a problem I need to solve."

"That's exactly why I think we need to take it slow," Grant said, smiling. "So as long as we all agree, I think we're all on the same page. Let's start sharing our ideas."

Nuria smiled back. "Let's do it!"

## ROADBLOCKS

*"WE LIVE TO LOVE, TO SERVE, AND TO LEAD OTHERS WITH PURPOSE AND IMPACT."*

CHAPTER 21

# OUR HEROES TAKE A NOVEL APPROACH TO IDENTIFYING ROADBLOCKS

**"GREAT,"** Grant continued, "I'll go first. I can think of four major roadblocks. First, as I mentioned just a little bit ago, my business can change almost on a dime if there's a big change in the direction of the stock market or the economy. Even though I try hard to help my clients understand that our financial plans can withstand whatever the markets may throw their way, it does cause some disruption. So I need to have a plan for giving my clients a little extra attention when things get tough.

"Second, there's a lot of new financial technology out there that some people think can replace the relationship that a client has with a financial planner. Of course, I don't believe that's true. I believe most people really need financial advice to help them stay on track. To keep them from getting too excited when things are going well and to keep them from getting too worried when things aren't going so well. Sometimes my role is more like a psychologist than an investment advisor. That means I need to find and maintain a good blend between personal advice and the technology I offer my clients. I must stay open to technological advances, or they can become a roadblock.

"Third, rules and regulations in my business are constantly changing. I can sometimes allow those rules to get in the way of growing my business. I spend too much time worrying about what I can't do, even if it's pretty minor in the grand scheme of things. Regulations may cause a lot of extra paperwork, but they should never stop me from serving my clients and executing my plans. And I have to remember that or it can become a roadblock.

"My final roadblock is the way that I sometimes deal with the open time slots on my calendar. That's time I should be scheduling for myself to work on important projects, but I know I tend to take free time for granted and blow it off. I need to be better at scheduling what will go into those time periods. Time blocking can become a roadblock."

"You came up with those pretty quickly," Bo remarked. "Seems like you've thought about them before."

"I have," Grant admitted. "I think it's part of my DNA as a financial planner. After all, risk management is a big part of what I do every day."

"What I heard," Nuria offered, "was you addressing those potential roadblocks from four different perspectives. First, you thought about outside threats caused by changing financial circumstances. Second, you looked at threats from the perspective of your competitive landscape. Third, you looked at potential changes in your industry, especially as it relates to compliance. And finally, you considered internal threats caused by a lack of consistent focus. That's a great way for all of us to consider the things that may be roadblocks to our personal and business development.

"For me," she continued, "I don't foresee any specific external roadblocks. Web design isn't as volatile as the financial markets. However, I do believe we may face obstacles related to competition.

My team operates like a local business, because we prefer clients within an hour or two of our office. While web design projects can be managed virtually, in-person meetings give us a competitive edge and strengthen our relationships. Unfortunately, more clients and potential clients are being approached by online-only competitors they'll never meet in person. Although I can emphasize our personal touch to our advantage, ignoring this trend could also become a roadblock.

"Of course, I'm in the technology business, so things are constantly changing; another of my potential roadblocks is if I don't keep myself and my team up to date on significant technological changes. I'm guessing I look at that like you look at new rules and regulations, Grant. It's not a roadblock unless I either ignore it completely or stress myself out too much about it.

"My greatest internal, or personal, roadblock is making sure I don't overdo it when it comes to looking for new ideas. Sometimes my daydreaming gets in the way of the time that I should be taking action on projects. It's like professional procrastination, because one of the things I enjoy most is thinking creatively. My innovative ideas help me set my business apart from the competition, and I don't ever want to run a cookie-cutter business, but I must remember there's a limit to the amount of time that I can spend thinking creatively before it gets in the way of actually running my business."

"I think you're both on the right track," Bo offered. "For me, I think my biggest roadblocks could be focus and concentration. Sure, there are outside threats, I definitely have competition, and the marketing world is constantly changing. But the thing that's always getting in my way when I'm feeling stuck is a loss of focus and concentration. Those are the two words I'm going to put on the back of my roadblock card. A simple reminder each day that I need to stay dialed into those things that I've committed to doing and avoid procrastination and distractions."

"I like that," Grant said. "I think those are two words that we should all keep in mind as we move forward."

"You know," Nuria said, "I think we could all benefit from shrinking down the descriptions of our roadblocks to keywords that will remind us of them. For me, those three words would be 'local,' 'innovation,' and, like Bo, 'concentration.' They remind me to think of my advantage of being a local provider, to be on the lookout for new innovations, and to concentrate on those things that I have set out to do through my TFAP."

"I like what you did there, Nuria," Grant said. "I'd like to take a crack at that myself. My words would be 'markets,' 'competition,' 'compliance,' and, also borrowing from Bo, 'focus.' I need to be aware of what's going on in the markets and how it may impact my business, never underestimate the competitive landscape, stay compliant with new rules and regulations, and focus on how I spend my time, especially time that I schedule with myself."

As Grant finished, Tito came back to the booth.

"How did you do?" he asked, and listened intently as they explained their conversation. "I have to admit," Tito replied, "that's a novel way of thinking about roadblocks, but I bet it will work. Especially since you'll be holding each other accountable through your roundtable. Remember, you can always make changes. One of the best attributes of a roundtable is adaptability. Situations change, people change, and you have to be willing to adapt so that you're always giving your best effort to the way you're serving each other."

"So what's next?" Grant asked.

"I think you're ready for graduation," Tito answered. "No homework this week, and next week we'll celebrate your graduation."

"That's not really true, though, is it?" Bo asked. "We do have homework; we need to continue to stay focused on our TFAPs. I'm sure you don't want us to take a week off from being Truest Fans."

"Caught me again," Tito replied. "I was trying to take a shortcut. What I meant is that I'm not going to give you any new assignments this week. I want you to put what we've been working on into further action. During next week's graduation ceremony I'll suggest a format for keeping your roundtable as strong as it can possibly be, even when I'm not formally teaching you anymore. How does that sound?"

"Can't wait," Nuria answered. "Will you be providing caps and gowns?"

"No," Tito replied, "but I may add some whipped cream and a cherry on top of your pancakes."

CHAPTER 22

# DISCOVERING INTENTIONALITY

**A FEW DAYS LATER,** Grant and Bo unexpectedly ran into each other at the coffee shop. After a quick hello, Grant asked, "How are you feeling about our upcoming graduation, Bo?"

"To be honest," Bo replied, "I don't think I'm happy about it at all. We've made great progress, and even though we know we can always go to Tito with questions, I wonder if we're really ready to go about this on our own."

"I feel the same way," Grant replied. "We've made a huge commitment to each other, and I don't want to let you all down."

"I don't think we'll let each other down intentionally," Bo replied. "But if we don't have a system for staying on track, especially during our breakfasts, things could go off the rails very quickly."

"That's a great point," Grant remarked. "We need to be intentional about this. If we're going to be each other's Truest Fans, we need to be intentional about the way we come together and the way we lead our lives."

"I couldn't agree more," Bo said. "I think we both admit that in the past we have not been as intentional as we've needed to be in our businesses. Our success has been wonderful, but it will be even better when we intentionally commit to being the best we can be."

"Absolutely," Grant agreed. "We need to be the best versions of ourselves."

"I think," Bo said, "we've all felt a little bit of the imposter syndrome as we've gone into this roundtable. We've questioned whether we actually deserve the success we've had, because in some ways it feels like it's come so easy, even though we know we've worked very hard over the years."

"Yes," Grant admitted. "We don't just need to live the life that we want to live. We need to intentionally live the life that we were meant to live. This whole idea of being a Truest Fan isn't just an exercise in time management or goal setting; it's a lifestyle where we genuinely commit to being our best so that we can better serve everyone around us: our clients, our families, and the causes we care about."

"Intentionally!" Bo exclaimed, marveling at how perfect the world felt. "I can't believe we haven't talked about intentionality before. This changes everything. If we're going to be the best versions of ourselves, we need to intentionally commit to it every single day."

CHAPTER 23

# SUCCESS, CHALLENGE, ACTION, SERVE

**WHEN THE TRIO ARRIVED** the following week, Tito was already waiting at the table. As they took their seats, he handed out the final Truest Fan cards, noticeably smaller than the previous ones and similar in size to a business card. The Truest Fan motto appeared at the bottom, as usual. The rest of the card had a distinct layout, with no space for writing. The top of the card displayed "Truest Fan Roundtable," followed by four numbered words: 1) Success, 2) Challenge, 3) Action, and 4) Serve.

"The most important thing that we need to do during today's graduation ceremony," Tito instructed, "is to create a framework for how you'll get the most out of your weekly roundtable breakfasts."

Bo interrupted, "I want to ask you a question, Tito."

Tito smiled. "Absolutely. What's on your mind, Bo?"

Bo explained what he and Grant had discussed a few days ago, about the importance of being intentional in chasing their goals.

"Incredible," Tito said with admiration. "Intentionality is at the heart of dreaming dreams, setting goals, and taking action. Without intentionality, everything we've been working on could simply fade into the background. We could end up going back to doing things the way we have in the past."

Nuria agreed. "I couldn't have said it better myself."

Tito wrote the word INTENTIONALITY in big letters on the back of Bo's card. "This is your insight, so you're going to be in charge of reminding the group to keep it in mind. Being a Truest Fan, continuously becoming a better version of yourself doesn't happen by accident. Your time together as a roundtable should reinforce that point. Greater and greater accountability leads to greater and greater intentionality."

Grant shared, "I for one plan to be more intentional in everything that I do. And I don't think I would have understood that if we hadn't taken the time to form this roundtable."

Tito smiled. "Good stuff. Are you about ready to graduate now?"

They all replied in unison, "Yes!"

"Tell us about the last card," Grant suggested. "I thought we would just talk about our TFAPs today."

"That's definitely a part of it," Tito replied. "So are your big dreams, Quick Wins, and Game Plans. And I'm sure you'll use the 4D Framework to dissect many of the things that you will discuss."

"My team has still been applying the 4D Framework to our meetings," Nuria offered. "We're using them in our daily stand-ups as well as our monthly planning sessions. The framework has proven to be invaluable. 4D helps inform our agenda."

"I really like the way you've taken that framework and run with it, Nuria," Tito affirmed, "and I hope you keep it up. The agenda we'll talk about today will make your roundtable meetings another step better."

"There's always room for improvement," Nuria replied.

"So," said Tito, "the best meetings always have an agenda. The words on your cards are yours. They'll shape your roundtable meetings each week. When you start your meetings, you'll go through the list one word at a time.

"First, you want to open the meeting by celebrating your success. You should each take a turn before you move on. Some weeks there may be big successes, and others there may only be small accomplishments. No matter what they are, it's important to share them. They're the fuel that puts the energy in your gatherings. They keep you from getting too bogged down in things that may be bothering you. Celebrate successes first."

"What if I had a bad week?" Grant asked. "After all, sometimes you just don't feel very successful."

"That probably means you're selling yourself short," Tito answered. "You just didn't take enough time to think about your blessings. In my experience, even in the worst of times there's a silver lining. And the best way to avoid stinking thinking is to head it off at the pass."

"I gotcha," Grant said. "I guess I was just looking for an excuse to stay down in the dumps. Misery loves company."

"No worries," Nuria chimed in. "We all get that way sometimes. And I'm glad our weekly roundtables we will help us avoid that temptation."

"Second," Tito continued, "you should each take time to talk about any challenges that you may have run into over the past week. You need to be careful; don't let your discussion of challenges turn into a gripe session. Challenges are things that are truly getting in the way of making progress. Challenges are not situations or people that raise your blood pressure. They're not the trivialities we sometimes feel we need to vent about. Your challenges are things that you truly need to get past to be able to move forward."

"Will we each run into challenges every week?" Bo asked.

"Probably not," Tito reassured, "but they happen, and you have to be ready to address them. Often, they relate to your roadblocks. Ignoring them and putting them off will never help you get through them. When you talk through them, you have a better chance of understanding why they occurred, and maybe even keeping them from happening again."

"That makes perfect sense," Nuria said. "And with the brain trust that we have at this table, I bet we'll be able to work through our challenges more efficiently than ever."

"Right on," Bo echoed. "After all, we are all in this together."

"Action is next," Tito continued. "Actions are the steps that you're going to take in the coming week to build on your successes, overcome any challenges that may be getting in your way, and act on new ideas that have surfaced that support your TFAP. Some weeks you may walk away with a handful of action items, and other weeks it may just be one or two. Ask yourself if the actions you're proposing support your TFAP, and if they do, you should move forward with them."

"Absolutely," Grant quipped. "After all, action-takers are money-makers."

"Listen," said Tito, "if that little catchphrase resonates with you, I'm happy to let you repeat it five times a day. Now, the fourth agenda item, my favorite, is serve. This is your chance to think about how you can serve others in the week ahead. You want to uncover anything you can do to help your partners keep moving on their TFAPs, plus anything that might help out your families, coworkers, and communities. Serving others is an essential part of being a Truest Fan."

"You know, I didn't think about that until just now," Grant said, "but for the last several weeks, I think we've all been exchanging calls, emails, and messages. Stuff comes up where we need a hand or have a question, or we just want to check in and see how the other person is doing. It's been great!"

"And I've only been answering those emails during my email inbox time," said Bo with a huge grin on his face.

"Funny," Nuria laughed, "I still think you're trying to edge everybody out for teacher's pet."

"Sounds like you're having fun with this," Tito said. "I'm glad you're not just restricting your Truest Fan Roundtable experience to these breakfasts. In the best roundtables, the partners become an almost integral part of each other's daily lives. After all, Truest Fans are supposed to be cheering each other on, and there's no timetable for that. That's why service is such an important weekly agenda item. It reminds you to stay on track with your priorities while still serving others, whether it's through the discussion you're having over breakfast or as things happen throughout the week."

As Tito was finishing his thoughts, one of his waiters set a huge pile of pancakes on the table with whipped cream and cherries on the top.

"I thought you were kidding," Bo joked.

"Well," Tito replied, "I was. And then I got to thinking about the many ways that you all have impacted my life as I've been working with you. You have blessed me by listening, being open to new ideas, and then putting them to work. I'm sure I've learned just as much as you have. For that, I'm grateful. You all deserve a treat."

"That calls for a toast," Grant offered. "Do you mind?"

They all nodded in agreement.

"Here's to loving and to serving others," Grant started, "and taking our call to be leaders seriously. So that we live with greater purpose, impacting the world by intentionally choosing to be Truest Fans whenever and wherever we can."

"Hear! Hear!" They all said, clinking their mugs and taking a big gulp of Tito's famous coffee.

**TRUEST FAN ROUNDTABLE**

**SUCCESS**

**CHALLENGE**

**ACTION**

**SERVE**

*"WE LIVE TO LOVE, TO SERVE, AND TO LEAD OTHERS WITH PURPOSE AND IMPACT."*

CHAPTER 24

# OUR HEROES ENJOY THEIR SUCCESS

**ABOUT THREE MONTHS LATER,** Nuria, Grant, and Bo were meeting for their regular Truest Fan Roundtable at Tito's Diner. They'd decided to use this particular session to review what they had accomplished since they had begun meeting. Besides, it was a good time to update their TFAPs.

Just as they were about to begin, Tito joined them at the table. "Do you mind if I sit in today?" he asked.

"Not at all," Grant replied. "As you probably heard, we have a different agenda for today's meeting. We're going to look back at how things have gone over the last several months. There's been a lot going on."

"Then this should be good," Tito said with excitement. "Who is going first?"

As usual, Bo was quick to jump in.

"I'll go," he said. "First off, because of the 4D Framework, I'm taking two Fridays off each month. I use one of those days to have a long weekend with my family and the other to work on a service project. Overall, I've been feeling much more energized and refreshed because I'm able to clear my mind when I'm away from the office.

"I've also added two new clients who are now my biggest financial relationships. More importantly, they're in the industries I enjoy serving most.

"My biggest challenge is keeping prospective clients like these in the pipeline. The sales cycle, even though it's more rewarding, takes longer. So I'm going to make some adjustments to my TFAP this quarter to make sure I'm serving these clients' needs and keeping them happy throughout the process."

"Awesome," Tito commented. "It sounds like you're continuing to learn and grow and make progress toward your big dreams."

"No doubt," Bo replied, "but wait till you hear what Nuria has accomplished."

"Are you trying to steal my thunder, Bo?" Nuria asked.

"Not at all, Nuria, I'm just so proud of you that I wanted to help set the stage."

"Thanks, Bo," Nuria said. "To begin, I must say, the last three months have been some of the most productive I've ever had. I can't ever remember feeling so excited about the many things that are going on in my business and with my family. I've also done something that I'd not even thought about when we first started meeting."

"Cut the suspense," Tito joked. "Please tell me what's going on."

"Last week, I signed a letter of intent to buy one of my competitors," Nuria said with great excitement. "As you know, that wasn't even part of my long-term big dreams. The new client that I took on during the first couple of weeks of our roundtable suggested to me that the firm she had fired could use some new leadership. She really liked the people at her former web design firm, but they had lost their way. She asked me if I would be willing to sit down with their CEO and just share how I run my company. I agreed; it was a simple favor. As good fortune would have it, the CEO and I hit it off from the start. He joked that he would like to come work for me. And the rest is history; I'm going to buy his company and he's going to join our team."

"You know," Grant interrupted, "even though that may not have been on your TFAP for this quarter, it definitely was part of your big dreams. I'm guessing this acquisition could be a big step toward building your business so you'll someday be able to sell it to your teammates. You're building the number of folks in your organization who can take on leadership roles as time moves along."

"That's absolutely right, Grant," Nuria replied. "As you know, it didn't take me long to decide to pursue this opportunity. Though this acquisition may have come much earlier than I could ever have imagined, it completely matches up with my plans for the future."

"One more question," Tito interrupted. "Did you ever decide where to take your big two-week vacation with your family?"

"You don't miss a thing, do you, Tito?" Nuria asked. "We decided to keep it simple. We rented a cabin on a secluded lake in Maine. We're just going to enjoy nature and being together."

"Sounds perfect," Tito replied. "How about you, Grant?"

"I've never felt better about my business," Grant answered. "I've added three new ideal clients, my pipeline is full, and I haven't worked a late night or on a Saturday in weeks. I'm feeling more energized and it's helping me feel more connected to my family."

"You all are doing great," Tito said. "I couldn't be happier."

"Well, you've been a big part of our success," Grant added.

"That's just what Truest Fans do," Tito said. "Remember, it's all about living to love and to lead so that your life has greater purpose. You make an impact on the world, beginning with the people you encounter each day. What you all are doing now is only the tip of the iceberg. I'm rooting for your continued success!"

# LEARN MORE

**THANK YOU** for taking the time to read *The Truest Fan Blueprint.* I hope that the ideas presented in this book have already started to make a positive impact on your life. I never imagined that I would write two books on this topic, but I am thrilled to share my passion for the Truest Fan approach with others. These books have been some of my big dreams coming true.

If you're looking for even more ways to implement the Truest Fan Blueprint, please visit TruestFan.com. There, you'll learn about my coaching and consulting services, gain access to my podcast, and find ways to form your own roundtable and become part of the Truest Fan community. Let's continue to support and encourage one another as we strive toward our big dreams.

# GOD IS OUR TRUEST FAN

**IF YOU'VE READ THIS BOOK** from the start, and you're not reading the last pages first, you've learned that your journey in business and life can be very lonely. That's true whether you work alone or you come together with others for a common purpose. A Truest Fan Roundtable, working with others to reach your big dreams, is a great way to eliminate that loneliness as you find other Truest Fans who will root you on to be your very best.

For me, as a Christian, I believe there is no greater Truest Fan than God. He will never leave us alone, He will always be with us. And whatever your specific beliefs, I would encourage you to include a higher power in your Truest Fan journey. In fact, lesson #6 of the original Truest Fan book states, "You are never alone. God is your Truest Fan."

In the Old Testament, Joshua teaches us, "Be strong and courageous; do not be frightened or dismayed, for the Lord your God is with you wherever you go" (Joshua 1:9 NIV). I firmly believe this to be true. As we build our businesses, grow our families, and go out into the world to serve others, He is with us.

# ABOUT THE AUTHOR

**ROB BROWN** has spent most of his career in the financial services industry as a top-producing advisor as well as in several senior leadership roles. Now, as a business coach, Rob helps his clients achieve excellence while living more purpose-filled lives. Rob is an author, devoted husband and father, and a lifelong Cleveland baseball fan. His first book, *Truest Fan: Live, Love, and Lead with Purpose and Impact*, received glowing reviews from CEOs, fellow business authors, and religious leaders alike.

Over the course of his career, Rob has discovered that a large part of his success has come through the active encouragement of others. Whether he's coaching, mentoring, speaking, or leading training events, he loves cheering on colleagues and clients.

www.ingramcontent.com/pod-product-compliance
Lightning Source LLC
Chambersburg PA
CBHW071421210326
41597CB00020B/3609

* 9 7 8 1 7 3 7 3 7 4 2 6 8 *